WHAT TH[E...]
THE JOB [...]

"... A superior series of jo[b...]"

**-Cornell University
Career Center
WHERE TO START**

"A timely book for Chicago job hunters follows books from the same publisher that were well received in New York and Boston...A fine tool for job hunters..."

**-Clarence Petersen
THE CHICAGO TRIBUNE**

"Job hunting is never fun, but this book can ease the ordeal...The Southern California Job Bank will help allay fears, build confidence and avoid wheel-spinning."

**-Robert W. Ross
THE LOS ANGELES TIMES**

"This well-researched, well-edited job hunter's aid includes most major businesses and institutional entities in the New York metropolitan area...Highly recommended."

**-Cheryl Gregory-Pindell
LIBRARY JOURNAL**

"Here's the book for your job hunt...Trying to get a job in New York? I would recommend a good look through the Metropolitan New York Job Bank..."

**-Maxwell Norton
NEW YORK POST**

"Help on the job hunt...Anyone who is job-hunting in the New York area can find a lot of useful ideas in a new paperback called The Metropolitan New York Job Bank..."

**-Angela Taylor
THE NEW YORK TIMES**

"If you are looking for a job...before you go to the newspapers and the help-wanted ads, listen to Bob Adams, editor of The Metropolitan New York Job Bank."

**-Tom Brokaw
NBC TELEVISION**

"No longer can job seekers feel secure about finding employment just through want ads. With the tough competition in the job market, particularly in the Boston area, they need much more help. For this reason, The Boston Job Bank will have a wide and appreciative audience of new graduates, job changers, and people relocating to Boston. It provides a good place to start a search for entry-level professional positions."

**-from a review in
THE JOURNAL OF
COLLEGE PLACEMENT**

What makes the JOB BANK SERIES the nation's premier line of employment guides:

With vital employment information on thousands of the nation's largest companies, the **JOB BANK SERIES** is the most comprehensive and authoritative set of career directories available today.

Each of the entries provides contact information, telephone numbers, addresses and a thumbnail sketch of the firm's business. Many entries also include a listing of the firm's typical professional job categories, the principal educational backgrounds sought, and the fringe benefits offered.

All of the reference information in the **JOB BANK SERIES** is as up-to-date and accurate as possible. Every year, the entire database is thoroughly researched and verified, first by mail and then by telephone. More local **JOB BANK** books come out more often than any other comparable publications.

In addition, the **JOB BANK SERIES** features important information about the local job scene--forecasts on which industries are the hottest, overviews of local economic trends, and even lists of regional professional associations, so you can get your job hunt started off right!

Looking for a particular kind of employer? Each **JOB BANK** Book features a comprehensive cross-index, which lists entries both by industry and, in multi-state job markets, by state. This means a person seeking a job in, say, finance, can identify major employers quickly and accurately.

Hundreds of discussions with job-hunters show they prefer information organized geographically, because most people look for jobs in specific areas. The **JOB BANK SERIES** offers sixteen regional titles, from Minneapolis to Houston, and from Washington, D.C., to San Francisco. The future employee moving to a particular area can review the local employment data and get a feel not only for the type of industry most common to that region, but also for major employers.

A condensed, but thorough, review of the entire job search process is presented in the chapter, 'The Basics of Job Winning', a feature that has received many compliments from career counselors. In addition, each **JOB BANK** directory is completed by a section on resumes and cover letters **The New York Times** has acclaimed as "excellent".

The **JOB BANK SERIES** gives job-hunters the most comprehensive, most timely, and most accurate career information, organized and indexed to facilitate the job search. An entire career reference library, **JOB BANK** books are the consummate employment guides.

Cover photograph courtesy of the Seattle Convention and Visitors Bureau.

Published by Bob Adams, Inc.
840 Summer Street, Boston MA 02127

Copyright © 1989 by Bob Adams, Inc. All rights reserved. No part of the material printed may be reproduced or utilized in any form or by any means, electronic or mechanical, including photo-copying, recording, or by any information storage retrieval system without written permission from the publisher.

The Seattle Job Bank, the briefcase logo, and the cover design are all trademarks of Bob Adams, Inc.

Brand name products mentioned in the employer listings are proprietary property of the applicable firm, subject to trademark protection, and registered with government offices.

While the publisher has made every reasonable attempt to obtain accurate information and verify same, occasional errors are inevitable due to the magnitude of the data base. Should you discover an error, please write the publisher so that corrections may be made in future editions.

The appearance of a listing anywhere in this book does not constitute an endorsement from the publisher.

Cover design by Brandon Toropov.

Manufactured in the United States of America.

ISBN: 1-55850-989-5

The Seattle Job Bank

Other top career publications from Bob Adams, Inc.:

The Atlanta Job Bank ($10.95)
The Boston Job Bank ($12.95)
The Dallas Job Bank ($12.95)
The Florida Job Bank ($12.95)
The Greater Chicago Job Bank ($12.95)
The Houston Job Bank ($12.95)
The Los Angeles Job Bank ($10.95)
The Metropolitan Washington (DC)
 Job Bank ($10.95)
The Minneapolis Job Bank ($12.95)
The New York Job Bank ($12.95)
The Ohio Job Bank ($10.95)
The Philadelphia Job Bank ($10.95)
The San Francisco Bay Area
 Job Bank ($12.95)
The St. Louis Job Bank ($12.95)

Careers and the MBA ($14.95)
Cold Calling Techniques
 That Really Work ($6.95)
The Consultant's Handbook ($12.95)
Hiring the Best ($9.95)
The Job Bank Guide to Employment
 Services (covers 50 states: $119.95)
The Job Search Handbook ($6.95)
Knock 'em Dead, with Great
 Answers to Tough Interview
 Questions ($6.95)
The National Job Bank (covers
 50 states: $179.95)

To order these books or additional copies of this book, send check or money order (including $2.75 for postage) to

Bob Adams, Inc., 840 Summer Street, Boston MA 02127.

Ordering by credit card?
Just Call 1-800-USA-JOBS toll free.
(In Massachusetts call 617/268-9570)

The Seattle Job Bank

Managing Editor: Carter Smith

Associate Editors: Lisa Teuscher, Linda Werbner

A copy of **The Seattle Job Bank** is one of the most effective weapons you can find for your professional job hunt. Use this guide for the most up-to-date information on most major businesses in the metropolitan Seattle area. It will supply you with specific addresses, phone numbers, and personnel contact information.

Separate yourself from the flock of candidates who answer the help-wanted advertisements, randomly hoping for a job. The method this book offers, direct employer contact, boasts twice the success rate of any other. Exploit it.

Read and use this book to uncover new opportunities. Here's how:

Formulate a target list of potential employers. The "Industry Cross-Index" section which breaks down companies by business segment, will help.

Consult the company listings in the "Primary Employer Listings" section. Use that information to supplement your own research, so you'll be knowledgeable about the firm --- before the interview.

Polish your job seeking strategy by reading the "Basics of Job Winning" section. It's a condensed review of the most effective job search methods.

Write a winning resume and learn how to sell yourself most effectively on paper. See the " Resumes and Cover Letters" section.

Use the "Professional Employment Services" section to put area employment specialists at your fingertips.

Learn more about trends in your industry and make important contacts by consulting the "Professional Associations" section.

The Seattle Job Bank will give you an idea of the incredible diversity of employment possibilities in one of the world's most dynamic business centers. Your ultimate success will depend largely on how vigorously you use the information provided within these pages. This unique employment guide can lead you to a company that otherwise has remained undiscovered. With a willingness to apply yourself, a winning attitude, and the headstart on your research that **The Seattle Job Bank** provides, you can obtain your career objective.

Table of Contents

1. INTRODUCTION/13

An informative economic outlook section that will help you understand the forces shaping the job market.

2. PRIMARY EMPLOYER LISTINGS/17

Includes the address, phone number, description of the company's basic product lines and services, and for most firms, the name of the contact person for professional positions.

3. INDUSTRY CROSS-INDEX/143

Local employers are cross-indexed by industrial category.

4. PROFESSIONAL EMPLOYMENT SERVICES/165

Includes names, addresses and primary areas of specialization for local executive search firms and employment agencies.

5. PROFESSIONAL ASSOCIATIONS/185

A special section, giving names and addresses of many of the area's professional trade associations.

6. THE BASICS OF JOB WINNING/211

A condensed review of the basic elements in a successful job search campaign. Includes advice on developing an effective strategy, time planning, preparing for interviews, interview techniques, etc.

7. RESUMES AND COVER LETTERS/237

Advice on and samples of resumes and cover letters

Introduction

THE SEATTLE JOB BANK

AN ECONOMIC OVERVIEW

Seattle is the population, employment and financial nerve center of the Northwest. Located on Puget Sound in northern Washington state, the city boasts a notably broad-based economy, centered around industrial manufacturing, international trade and a service sector.

The international trade segment of Seattle's economy is bolstered by the city's role as a major port of call. A veritable reservoir of prosperity, the port of Seattle handles the second largest amount of container cargo in the country. To augment this success, the city has recently sanctioned $100 million terminal improvements program in order to meet ever-increasing trade with the Far East Geographically, Seattle is about one and a half days closer to the Orient than the West Coast competing ports in Oakland and Long Beach and is ordinarily the first American seaport visited by vessels from Hong Kong, Korea and Taiwan.

In addition to serving as an focal point for international trade, Seattle is also a center for the aerospace, forest products, food products, agricultural goods and primary metals industries.

The importance of the aerospace industry to the Seattle economy is well-known. Since 1983, the Boeing Company has added 33,000 new jobs, more than 8,000 of them in the past year. Not suprisingly, Boeing is by far the area's largest employer, providing work for one out of every ten workers in the Seattle-Tacoma region. The company has singlehandedly brought on the city's mid-1980s economic boom with total company employment climbing from 57,000 in 1983 to 80,000 in 1986.

Reliance on one industry, much less one corporation, can, however be flirting with trouble. Since over 40 percent of Boeing's sales come from contracted government work, the area's economic planners must be prepared for cutbacks in government contracts, especially in these times of tight fiscal restraint.

An interesting way to get a clearer picture of Seattle's economy is to compare the regional economy during the 1980s with that of the nation as a whole. Washington follows but does not mirror national trends. The 1980-82 recession hit the Pacific Northwest disproportionately; while national employment dropped 3 percent, employment in Washington fell 5 percent. According to the Seattle Chamber of Commerce, Washington lost 90,000 out of 1.7 million jobs.

Recovery also took longer to recover. It took the United States one year to recover, while Washington took a year and a half.

At the same time, the state was not hurt as badly as some of its neighbors.

Since 1983, the nation has added 16 percent to its employment rolls. During the same period, Washington, led by the greater Seattle area, increased employment by 18 percent. Growth in 1987 was strong and well-balanced, with few industries showing losses.

The positive trend continued into 1988. According to the U.S Department of Labor's Bureau of Labor Statistics, unemployment dropped from 5.9 percent in July, 1987 to 4.6 percent by August, 1988.

Part of the reason for this drop has to do with one factor that sets Seattle's economy apart from most of the rest nation -- manufacturing employment is actually growing, not shrinking. While much of the country still lags 10 percent below their pre-early 1980s recession peaks in manufacturing employment, the state of Washington actually experienced a 7.4-percent increase in manufacturing jobs, which meant about 12,900 new jobs. Granted, most of these gains were the 8,800 new people employed in aerospace manufacturing, but only two manufacturing industries registered losses from November 1986 to November 1987 -- the category "other transportation equipment" and the apparel category lost a total of 800 jobs.

Non-manufacturing employment increased by 29,800 - a 4.1-percent increase over the year. Largest contributors to this sector's employment gains were wholesale/retail trade - 12,900 new jobs - and services - 16,300 new jobs. Only one non-manufacturing industry showed a decrease, as government reduced its workforce by 0.9 percent.

In another positive sign of economic strength, downtown Seattle's construction industry offers great opportunity for job seekers. Major projects include a new transit tunnel to link Highway I-90 with downtown, and the $136 million Washington State Convention Center. Thirteen new buildings, which will add of 6.6 million square feet of office space, are being built or are in the design stages. Analysts believe that despite current double-digit office vacancy rates, Seattle will absorb the newly created space as the city maintains it expansion.

Primary Employer Listings

THE SEATTLE JOB BANK

ABAM ENGINEERS, INC.
33301 Ninth Avenue South, Federal Way WA 98003. 206/952-6100. Contact Personnel Administrator. A consulting and civil engineering firm specializing in the design of piers and waterfront structures, tanks and reservoirs, bridges, transit guideways, buildings, floating structures and offshore drilling platforms. In addition to design, the firm performs concrete material research, advanced computer design analysis, and construction management. Corporate headquarters location. Common positions include: Accountant; Draftsperson; Civil Engineer; Marketing Specialist; Structural Engineer. Principal educational backgrounds sought: Accounting; Business Administration; Computer Science; Engineering; Marketing. Company benefits include: medical insurance; dental insurance; life insurance; tuition assistance; disability coverage.

ACKERLY COMMUNICATIONS, INC.
800 5th Avenue Suite 3770, Seattle WA 98104. 206/624-2888. Contact Personnel Department. A key Seattle company engaged in outdoor and airport advertising, professional basketball club, TV broadcasting, and real estate agents and brokers.

ACME POULTRY COMPANY, INC.
P.O. Box 3065, Seattle WA 98114. 206/324-8992. Contact Bob Boprey, Sales Manager. An area processor of poultry and related food products.

ACRO-WOOD
P.O. Box 1028, Everett WA 98206. 206/258-3555. Contact Philip Hutmacher, Controller. A pulp and

paper mill offering a variety of services and products to area customers, including plywood, particle board, and machinery for the lumber industry. Corporate headquarters location: New York, NY.

ADVANCED TECHNOLOGY LABORATORIES, INC.
P.O. Box 3003, Bothell WA 98041. 206/487-7416. Contact Personnel Manager. Engaged in the production and manufacture of a variety of electronic diagnostic equipment for use in medicine. Products include scanners and ultrasound systems.

AETNA LIFE & CASUALTY
1501 4th Avenue, Suite 800, Seattle WA 98101. 206/467-2500. Contact George C. Kelley, Marketing Manager. A company which maintains regional branch operations for the major national insurance firm. Oversees the marketing of insurance products, underwriting, casualty, and claims on all lines. Operations at this facility include: administration; service; sales. Corporate headquarters location: Hartford, CT. New York Stock Exchange. Common positions include: Claim Representative; Insurance Agent/Broker; Marketing Specialist; Underwriter. Principal educational backgrounds sought: Business Administration; Marketing. Company benefits include: medical insurance; dental insurance; pension plan; life insurance; tuition assistance; disability coverage; savings plan.

AGENA CORPORATION
9709 Third Avenue North East, Seattle WA 98115. 206/547-5226. Contact Personnel Department. A

principal independent insurance agent of automation services.

AIMSCO, INC.
4000-4024 22nd Avenue, West, P.O. Box 99056, Seattle WA 98119. 206/284-5563. Contact Personnel Department. A manufacturer of fasteners.

AIR VAN LINES
P.O. Box 3447, Bellevue WA 98009. 206/453-5560. Contact Personnel Director. A freight forwarding company with operations in domestic moving services.

AIRBORNE FREIGHT CORPORATION
3101 Western Avenue, P.O. Box 662/98111, Seattle WA 98121. 206/285-4600. Contact Personnel Department. An air express service.

ALASKA AIRLINES, INC.
19300 Pacific Highway South, P.O. Box 68900, Seattle WA 98188. 206/433-3200. Contact Personnel Department. A major air transportation service, tours, and cargo.

ALASKA NORTHWEST PUBLISHING COMPANY
130 Second Avenue South, Edmonds WA 98020. 206/774-4111. Contact Robert Henning, Publisher/Owner. An area publisher specializing in books relating to Alaska, including field guides.

ALASKA PACIFIC FISHERIES, INC.
2408 Commodore Way, Seattle WA 98199. 206/281-8778. Contact Personnel Department. A primary

Seattle fishery engaged in the processing of salmon and herring, and involved in boat chartering.

ALASKAN COPPER WORKS
3223 Sixth Avenue South, Seattle WA 98134. 206/623-5800, extension 558. Contact Ian Walker, Personnel Director. A producer of fabricated pipe and other metals products, including heat exchangers and process equipment. A division of Alaskan Copper Companies. Common positions include: Accountant; Administrator; Blue-Collar Worker Supervisor; Buyer; Credit Manager; Draftsperson; Engineer; Financial Analyst; Personnel & Labor Relations Specialist; Purchasing Agent; Sales Representative. Principal educational backgrounds sought: Accounting; Business Administration; Engineering; Finance; Marketing. Company benefits include: medical insurance; dental insurance; life insurance; disability coverage; profit sharing.

ALEXANDER & VENTURA
1215 Seneca Street, Seattle WA 98101. 206/622-2552. Contact Personnel Department. A prime Seattle company involved in operative building of multi-family dwellings and commercial buildings.

✷ ALLSTATE SEATTLE REGIONAL OPERATIONS CENTER
10330 Meridian North, Seattle WA 98133. 206/527-5550. Contact Division Personnel Manager. A member of the Sears Financial Network. One of the nation's largest insurance companies, handling life, health, commercial, and personal property lines of insurance.

This facility services the accounts of nine western states. Regional headquarters location. Common positions include: Computer Operator, Customer Service Representative; Department Manager; Division Manager; Unit Manager; Unit Supervisor; Management Trainee; Data Entry Clerks, Raters, Examiners; Management Trainee; Operations/Production Manager; Quality Control Supervisor. Principal educational backgrounds sought: Accounting; Business Administration; Communications; Economics; Finance. Company benefits include: medical insurance; pension plan; life insurance; tuition assistance; disability coverage; profit sharing; employee discounts; savings plan; dental plan.

AMERICAN PASSAGE MEDIA CORPORATION
500 Third Avenue, West, Seattle WA 98119. 206/282-8111. Contact Personnel Department. A major media firm providing media services to national advertisers interested in targeting specific market segments. The focus is on the youth market, the college segment in particular.

AMERICAN PLYWOOD ASSOCIATION
7011 S. 19th Street, Tacoma WA 98466. 206/565-6600. Contact Personnel Department. A construction and industrial panels, interior and exterior types and grades company.

AMERICAN SIGN AND INDICATOR CORPORATION
North 2310 Fancher Way, Spokane WA 99212. 509/535-4101. Contact Janet Hockersmith, Personnel

Director. The manufacturer of a variety of electronic and electric information display equipment, including scoreboards, advertising media, and transport terminal arrival/departure boards.

ARTHUR ANDERSEN & COMPANY
Norton Building, 801 Second Avenue, Seattle WA 98104. 206/623-8023. Contact Preston Prudente, Personnel Director. A major certified public accounting firm with offices in 40 countries worldwide. Company is divided into the following divisions: Audit, Tax, and Management Information Consulting. Audit division offers assignments in all types of businesses and industries; company offers a highly recognized professional development program in all phases of the industry. The Tax division offers assignments involving consultation and compliance in all areas of taxation including income, estate, trust, and gift taxation. Extensive professional development programs and the opportunity to obtain audit experience for the CPA certificate is provided. The Management Information Consulting Division offers opportunities for both entry-level and experienced personnel in providing professional systems and consulting services to a wide range of businesses and clients. Offers extensive formal training in information systems design and installation skills, and in business planning and reporting techniques. Corporate headquarters location: Chicago, IL.

ANGEL LEE, INC.
3211 South 154th, Seattle WA 98188. 206/243-8011. Contact Personnel Department. A leading Seattle

transportation company specializing in daily car rentals and airport parking.

ANIXTER-SEATTLE
18435 Olympic South, Seattle WA 98188. 206/251-5287. Contact Gary Richardson, Operations Manager. A diversified corporation with operations nationally in communications equipment, shipbuilding and related activities, and energy and natural resources operations. Corporate headquarters location: Skokie, IL.

AP DEVELOPMENT, INC.
3000 Rainier Tower, Seattle WA 98101. 206/682-6400. Contact Personnel Department. A primary management consultant service.]

APPLIED MICROSYSTEMS CORPORATION
5020 148th Avenue, North East, P.O. Box 97002, Redmond WA 98073-9702. 206/882-2000. Contact Gale D. Mowrer, Human Resource Department. Leading manufacturer and supplier of high quality software development tools and in-circuit emulators for embedded system development. Common positions include: Accountant; Buyer; Electrical Engineer. Company benefits include: medical, dental, and life insurance; tuition assistance; disability coverage. Corporate headquarters. Operations at this facility include: manufacturing; research/development; administration; service.

ARCO PETROLEUM PRODUCTS
7901-168th Avenue Northeast, Redmond WA 98052. 206/881-2113. Contact Personnel Director. A prime

resource recovery company, specializing in exploration and production of crude oil and natural gas, also petroleum products and petrochemical feed stocks.

ARMY CORPS OF ENGINEERS, WALLA WALLA DISTRICT DEPARTMENT OF THE ARMY
City County Airport, Bldg. 602, Walla Walla WA 99362-9265. Mailed inquires only. Contact Mr. Robert L. Alley, Chief recruitment and placement branch. A federal government agency, water resource engineering.

ASSOCIATED GROCERS, INC.
3301 South Norfolk, P.O. Box 3763, Seattle WA 98124. 206/762-2100. Contact Debbie Farris, Personnel Specialist. The Provider of general merchandise and grocery products to over 300 independently owned retail markets in a number of western states. Also offers a variety of related services including retail promotion. Employs over 1,000 people. Corporate headquarters location.

ATLANTIC RICHFIELD COMPANY
P.O. Box 1127, Cherry Point, Ferndale WA 98248. 206/384-1500. Contact Tony Mickas, Personnel Director. An energy products manufacturer engaged in the production of diesel and jet fuel, gasoline, and related petroleum products.

ATLAS FOUNDRY & MACHINE COMPANY
P.O. Box 11106, Tacoma WA 98411. 206/475-4600. Contact E. Russ Bodge, Personnel Director. The producer of a diversified range of steel and stainless

steel castings for the construction, transportation, maritime, oil, nuclear, and other industries. The firm also has fabrication and machining capabilities in large, complex weldments and castings. Corporate headquarters location. Common positions include: Accountant; Administrator; Blue-Collar Worker Supervisor; Buyer; Computer Programmer; Customer Service Representative; Ceramics Engineer; Metallurgical Engineer; Department Manager; Operations/Production Manager; Personnel & Labor Relations Specialist; Purchasing Agent; Quality Control Supervisor. Principal educational background sought: Engineering. Company benefits include: medical insurance; dental insurance; pension plan; life insurance; tuition assistance; disability coverage.

ATTACHMATE CORPORATION
13231 South East 36th Street, Bellevue WA 98006. 206/644-4010. Contact Julia Pritt, Secretary-Treasurer. A manufacturer of high technology and information processing components and support products, including PC expansion boards and data communication equipment.

AUDIO GROUP, INC.
200 South Orcas Street, Seattle WA 98108. 206/763-2517. Contact Personnel Department. A major Seattle company engaged in business services and electrical work contracting.

AUGAT COMMUNICATIONS GROUP, INC.
2414 South West Andover, Seattle WA 98106. 206/223-1110. Contact Personnel Department. A premier

Seattle manufacturer of telephone and telegraph apparatus. A division of Telzon, Inc.

AUTO CHLOR SYSTEM OF WASHINGTON
4315 7th Avenue South Seattle WA 98108. 206/622-0900. Contact Personnel Department. A primary Seattle company engaged in the wholesale and retail of chemicals. Also provides dishwashing services.

AVTECH CORPORATION
3400 Wallingford North, Seattle WA 98103. 206/634-2544. Contact Stan Hirooka, Personnel Director. A company which manufactures a variety of electronics equipment products for a number of end uses.

BANK OF PUGET SOUND
P.O. Box 90, Seattle WA 98111. 206/684-6000. Contact Personnel Department. The office of a leading Seattle bank.

BARDAHL MANUFACTURING CORPORATION
1400 North West 52nd, P.O. Box 70607, Seattle WA 98107. 206/783-4851. Contact Personnel Department. The producer of Bardahl additives & lubricants.

BARDIN FARMS CORPORATION
3887 Pioneer Way, P.O. Box 223, Monitor WA 98836. 509/782-3511. Contact Lyman Bardin, President. An area fruit processor; products include pears and apples.

E.J. BARTELLS COMPANY
P.O. Box 997, Renton WA 98057. 206/228-4111. Contact Personnel Director. A manufacturer of industrial insulation products and refractories.

EDDIE BAUER, INC.
15010 Northeast 36th Street, Redmond WA 98052. 206/882-6341. Contact Deborah Melzer, Director/Human Resources. A specialty retailer and mail order company offering outdoors gear and apparel to customers throughout the United States. A subsidiary of General Mills Inc. (Minneapolis, MN). Principal educational backgrounds sought: Accounting; Art/Design; Business Administration; Communications; Finance; Marketing. Company benefits include: medical insurance; dental insurance; pension plan; life insurance; tuition assistance; disability coverage; profit sharing; employee discounts; savings plan.

BAUGH CONSTRUCTION COMPANY
P.O.Box C, 14135, Seattle WA 98114. 206/447-2000. Contact Operations Department. An area commercial and industrial general contractor. Corporate headquarters location. Common positions include: Accountant; Construction Manager. Principal educational backgrounds sought: Business Administration; Construction Management; Engineering. Company benefits include: medical insurance; life insurance; profit sharing.

ROBERT E. BAYLEY CONSTRUCTION
1601 One Union Square, Seattle WA 98101. 206/621-8884. Contact Personnel Department. A general

building contractor, also specializing in commercial construction.

BAYLINER MARINE CORPORATION
P.O. Box 24467, Seattle WA 98124. 206/435-5571. Contact Pam Harkin, Personnel Director. A Seattle firm engaged in boat building activities. Employs over 800 people.

RW BECK & ASSOCIATES
2121 Fourth Avenue, Suite 600, Seattle WA 98121. 206/441-7500. Contact Personnel Department. A primary Seattle company engaged in engineering planning, management consulting and information, economic and operation analysis services.

BEKINS MOVING & STORAGE COMPANY
P.O. Box 30728, Seattle WA 98103-0728. 206/527-7600. Contact Personnel Director. A company whose services include the transportation and warehousing of household goods, office and industrial equipment, electronics, business records, and air freight forwarding. Corporate headquarters location: Glendale, CA.

BELL INDUSTRIES/
FARWEST MANUFACTURING DIVISION
18225 Northeast 76th, Redmond WA 98052. 206/885-4353. Contact Human Resource Administrator. Nationally, company is primarily a distributor of electronic components and a manufacturer of uncoated aluminum memory discs and other computer and electronic components. Also distributes building and construction, graphic arts and automotive products.

Common positions include: Accountant; Blue-Collar Worker Supervisor; Draftsperson; Industrial Engineer; Mechanical Engineer; Marketing Specialist; Quality Control Supervisor; Sales Representative; Technical Writer/Editor. Principal educational backgrounds sought: Business Administration; Engineering; Finance; Marketing. Company benefits include medical insurance; dental insurance; pension plan; life insurance; tuition assistance; disability coverage; profit sharing; savings plan. Corporate headquarters location: Los Angeles, CA. Operations at this facility include: manufacturing. New York Stock Exchange.

BELL-ANDERSON REALTY, INC.
25230 104th Southeast, Kent WA 98031. 206/852-8180. Contact Carlene Belton, Personnel Director. A provider of real estate and related services to area customers.

BELLINGHAM HERALD
1155 North State Street, Bellingham WA 98225. 206/676-2600. Contact Chet Young, Personnel Director. Operates an evening newspaper with circulation over 22,000. A member of the Gannett Newspapers Group.

BELSHAW BROTHER, INC.
1750 22nd South, Seattle WA 98144. 206/322-5474. Contact Personnel Department. A main bakery equipment manufacturer, products include donut robot, type k, multi-matic, batterboy, cut-n-fry, robot fri.

THE SEATTLE JOB BANK

BENAROYA SECURITIES COMPANY
1001 4th Avenue, Seattle WA 98154. 206/622-4750. Contact Personnel Department. A leading securities brokerage firm in the Seattle area.

BERING ENTERPRISES LTD. PARTNERSHIP
Fishermen's Center, Seattle WA 98119. 206/282-3445. Contact Personnel Department. A prominent Seattle company engaged in commercial fishing.

BIDDLE & CROWTHER COMPANY
910 North 137th, Seattle WA 98133. 206/365-9900. Contact Personnel Department. A prime Seattle company engaged in the wholesale of medical and surgical supplies and equipment.

BLUE CROSS OF WASHINGTON AND ALASKA
15700 Dayton North, Seattle WA 98133. 206/361-3000. Contact Personnel. A non-profit health care insurance organization offering a wide range of medical services to subscribers.

BOEING AEROSPACE COMPANY
P.O. Box 3999, Seattle WA 98124. 206/655-1131. Contact Personnel Department. The manufacturer of aerospace, aircraft, and electronic systems for commercial and military applications.

THE BOEING COMPANY
P.O. Box 3707, Mail Stop 31-13, Seattle WA 98124. 206/241-3300. Contact Employment Office. A company which manufactures aerospace, aircraft, and electronic systems for commercial and military

applications. Corporate headquarters location. Common positions include: Computer Programmer; Aerospace Engineer; Electrical Engineer; Mechanical Engineer; Metallurgical Engineer; Systems Analyst. Principal educational backgrounds sought: Engineering; Mathematics; Physics. Company benefits include: medical insurance; dental insurance; pension plan; life insurance; tuition assistance.

BOEING COMPUTER SERVICE COMPANY
P.O. Box 24346, Seattle WA 24346. 206/655-1131. Contact Personnel Department. A manufacturer aerospace, aircraft, and electronic systems for commercial and military applications.

THE BON
1601 Third & Pine, Seattle WA 98111. 206/344-2121. Contact Andrea Hoffield, Personnel Director. An area department store featuring a wide variety of quality merchandise.

BORDERS, PERRIN & NORRANDER
115 First Avenue, Seattle WA 98101. 206/343-7741. Contact Personnel Department. A major Seattle advertising agency.

BOVAY ENGINEERS, INC.
East 808 Sprague Avenue, Spokane WA 99202. 509/838-4111. Contact Sandra Trotter, Accounting Manager. A diversified systems engineering organization with activities in feasibility, environmental, and economic studies; master planning; site selection;

systems design; and many other areas. Corporate headquarters location: Houston, TX.

BRANOM INSTRUMENT COMPANY
5500 4th Avenue South, Seattle WA 98108. 206/762-6050. Contact Personnel Department. A key Seattle wholesaler of electronic parts and equipment.

BRAZIER FOREST INDUSTRIES, INC.
10828 Gravelly Lake Drive Southwest, P.O. Box 9945, Suite 211, Tacoma WA 98499. 206/584-1575. Contact Barbara Seiter, Personnel Director. A producer of a line of forest products, including plywood and lumber.

THE BREMERTON SUN
545 Fifth Street, P.O. Box 259, Bremerton WA 98310. 206/377-3711. Contact Ron Muhleman, Personnel Director. The publisher of an area evening newspaper, with a circulation of over 35,000. A member of the Scripps Newspapers Group.

BREMS EASTMAN
3131 Elliott Avenue Suite 280, Seattle WA 98121. 206/284-9400. Contact Personnel Department. A leading advertising agency.

BEN BRIDGE CORPORATION
1101 Pike Street, Seattle WA 98111. 206/628-6870. Contact Personnel Department. A key Seattle retailer of jewelry.

THE SEATTLE JOB BANK

BROWN AND CALDWELL
100 West Harrison Street, Seattle WA 98119. 206/281-4000. Contact Personnel Director. A nation wide consulting firm offering, technical services in environmental and engineering, planning, design, and construction management.

GORDON BROWN, INC.
P.O. Box 18225, Seattle WA 98118. 206/722-2100. Contact Personnel Department. A main Seattle company engaged in drywall plastering and accoustical tile contracting.

JOHN BROWN & PARTNERS
108 1st Avenue South, Seattle WA 98104. 206/622-9306. Contact Personnel Department. A major Seattle advertising agency.

BRYN MAWR PROPERTIES
11448 Rainier Avenue South, Seattle WA 98101. 206/772-0299. Contact Personnel Department. The operation and real estate managers of multi-family housing units.

BUFFELEN WOODWORKING COMPANY
P.O. Box 1383, Tacoma WA 98401. 206/627-1191. Contact Mr. Phillips, Personnel Director. A manufacturer of a variety of millwork and home lumber products, including plywood.

BURLINGTON NORTHERN, INC.
999 3rd Avenue, Seattle WA 98104-4097. 206/467-3838. Contact Personnel Department. A leading company

involved in railroad transportation of wholesale timber and logs, the manufacturing of forest products, crude oil and natural gas, as well as real estate sales and rentals.

BUSINESS SPACE DESIGN
111 South Jackson, Seattle WA 98104. 206/223-5000. Contact Mike Kreis, Personnel Director. An interior architecture services firm handling projects from single-office interiors to the planning and implementation of large office buildings, hotels, restaurants, health care, and government facilities in the U.S. and abroad. Parent company: The NBBJ Group (Seattle, WA). Common positions include: Architect; Draftsperson. Principal educational background sought: Interior Design. Company benefits include: medical insurance; pension plan; profit sharing. Corporate headquarters location. Operations at this facility include: sales.

CABLE HOUSE & RAGEN
999 Third Avenue Suite 4300, Seattle WA 98104. 206/343-5000. Contact Personnel Department. A leading Seattle company engaged in investment banking.

CALLISON PARTNERSHIP LTD.
1423 Third Avenue, Suite 300, Seattle WA 98101. 206/623-4646. Contact Personnel Department. A primary Seattle company involved in architectural interior design and space planning and programming.

THE SEATTLE JOB BANK

CAMAS MILL DIVISION/ CROWN ZELLERBACH
Northeast 4th and Adams, Camas WA 98607. 206/834-3021. Contact Richard Porter, Personnel Director. A manufacturer paper products and related goods as a division of Crown Zellerbach Corporation. Corporate headquarters location: San Francisco, CA. New York Stock Exchange.

CAPITAL DEVELOPMENT COMPANY
Four South Sound Center, Lacey WA 98503. 206/491-6850. Contact Gary Blume, Executive Vice-President. A company engaged in a variety of construction activities, including contracting, leasing, and property development and management. Other activities include lumber resource development.

CAPITAL INDUSTRIES, INC.
P.O. Box 80983, Seattle WA 98108. 206/762-8585. Contact Personnel Department. A principal Seattle company engaged in metal fabrication.

CARNATION COMPANY
2746 Northeast 45th Avenue, Seattle WA 98105. 206/527-7400. Contact Larry Allan, Office Manager. Nationally, the firm is a major manufacturer of food products, pet foods, animal feeds, scholastic materials, containers, and dietary products. Corporate headquarters location: Los Angeles, CA. New York Stock Exchange.

THE SEATTLE JOB BANK

CASCADE NATURAL GAS CORPORATION
222 Fair View Avenue North, Seattle WA 98109. 206/624-3900. Contact Mr. Fran Dols, Personnel Director. An area firm engaged in the distribution and transport of natural gas to customers. Common positions include: Accountant; Attorney; Claim Representative; Computer Programmer; Credit Manager; Customer Service Representative; Draftsperson; Economist; Mechanical Engineer; Department Manager; Marketing Specialist; Personnel & Labor Relations Specialist; Purchasing Agent; Statistician; Systems Analyst. Principal educational backgrounds sought: Accounting; Business Administration; Economics; Engineering; Finance; Mathematics. Company benefits include: medical insurance; dental insurance; pension plan; life insurance; tuition assistance; disability coverage. Operations at this facility include: administration. New York Stock Exchange.

✴ CEDARCREST ADVERTISING
576 116th Avenue North East, Bellevue WA 98004. . Contact Personnel Department. A major Bellevue advertising agency.

CENTURY 21 PROMOTIONS, INC.
2601 West Commodore Way, Seattle WA 98199. 1-800-426-7645. Contact Personnel Department. A leading importer of hats, caps, and jackets.

CHEF REDDY FOODS CORPORATION
P.O. Box 607, Othello WA 99344. 509/488-9611. Contact Personnel. A major processor of prepared

potato products, including potato rounds and french fries. Employs over 500 people.

CHRISTENSON RABER KIEF ASSOCIATION
P.O. Box 3923, Seattle WA 98124. 206/762-4215. Contact Personnel Department. A prominent Seattle construction company engaged in non residential building construction, heavy construction, and contracting.

CHUGACH FISHERIES, INC.
4241 21st West Suite 204, Seattle WA 98199. 206/284-0804. Contact Personnel Department. A leading Seattle company engaged in the wholesale, the processing, and the freezing of seafood and fish.

CLARK/WHITE & ASSOCIATES
505 North Riverside Suite 300, Spokane WA 99201. 509/747-6767. Contact Personnel Department. A leading Spokane advertising agency.

WILLIAM B. CLOES
8214 Greenwood North, Seattle WA 98103. 206/782-3131. Contact Personnel Department. A prominent retailer of womens ready to wear clothing, furniture and used merchandise.

CN DATA PROCESSING
10700 Meridian North, Seattle WA 98133. 206/367-5291. Contact Personnel Department. A prime Seattle company engaged in bank data processing.

COCHRAN ELECTRIC COMPANY, INC.

P.O. Box 33524, Seattle WA 98133-0524. 206/367-1900. Contact Personnel Department. A company involved in commercial and industrial electrical work and power-line engineering.

COLDWELL BANKER

1600 Park Place Building, Seattle WA 98101. 206/292-1600. Contact Maureen Ottele, Administrative Manager. Nationally, the firm is a major real estate service company with more than 17,800 employees and 680 offices from coast to coast. Founded in San Francisco in 1906, the firm is a fully-integrated real estate and real-estate-related service company with offices in major cities of the United States and Canada. Corporate headquarters location: Los Angeles, CA.

COLE & WEBER, INC.

308 Occidental Avenue South Seattle WA 98104. 206/447-9595. Contact Personnel Department. A prominent advertising and public relations agency.

COLUMBIA BASIN HERALD

813 West 3rd Avenue, P.O. Box 910, Moses Lake WA 98837. 509/765-4561. Contact Patrick Webb, Managing Editor. The publisher of an area newspaper with a circulation of over 7,000.

COLUMBIA LIGHTING, INC./ LIGHTING PRODUCTS GROUP

T.A. Box 2787, Spokane Industrial Park, Spokane WA 99220. 509/924-7000. Contact Frank Lydon, Personnel

Director. A manufacturer of lighting equipment for industrial and business applications.

COLUMBIA MACHINE, INC.
107 Grand Boulevard, Vancouver WA 98661. 206/694-1501. Contact Dolores Husebye, Personnel Director. A manufacturer of a variety of industrial machinery, steel products, and materials handling items. Employs over 500 people.

THE COLUMBIAN NEWSPAPER AND COMMERCIAL PRINTING COMPANY
701 West 8th Street, P.O. Box 180, Vancouver WA 98666. 206/694-3391. Contact Ann Michael, V.P. of Human Resources. A locally-owned, six-day-a-week newspaper serving Clark County, Washington. Circulation is 47,000. The firm's commercial printing division prints circulars and flyers. Corporate headquarters location. Operations at this facility include: manufacturing; administration; service; sales. Common positions include: Accountant; Advertising Worker; Blue-Collar Worker Supervisor; Commercial Artist; Computer Programmer; Credit Manager; Customer Service Representative; Department Manager; Operations/Production Manager; Personnel & Labor Relations Specialist; Programmer; Public Relations Worker; Purchasing Agent; Reporter/Editor; Sales Representative; Systems Analyst; Transportation & Traffic Specialist. Principal educational backgrounds sought: Accounting; Art/Design; Business Administration; Communications; Computer Science; Finance; Liberal Arts; Marketing. Company benefits include: medical insurance; dental insurance; life

insurance; tuition assistance; disability coverage; profit sharing; employee discounts.

COMINCO AMERICAN, INC.
P.O. Box 3087, Spokane WA 99220. 509/747-6111. Contact Personnel Director. A natural resource company engaged in a wide variety of activities, including mineral development, metals mining and marketing, and fertilizer production.

CONCRETE TECHNOLOGY CORPORATION
1123 Port of Tacoma Road, P.O. Box 2259, Tacoma WA 98401. 206/383-3545. Contact Personnel Director. A producer of concrete for a variety of end applications.

CONSOLIDATED FREIGHTWAYS
P.O. Box 3585, Seattle WA 98124. 206/763-1517. Contact Gene Owen, Personnel Director. A company which provides freight forwarding services to a variety of customers.

CONTAINER CORPORATION OF AMERICA
AN AFFILIATE OF JEFFERSON SMURFIT CORP.
P.O. Box 479, Renton WA 98057. 206/235-3300. Contact John Gardner, Employee Relations Manager. A major national producer of paperboard packaging. Manufacturing facilities are located throughout the United States and in foreign locations. Some major products include shipping containers, folding cartons, plastic drums, and many others. Corporate headquarters location: St. Louis, MO.

CONTINENTAL BAKING COMPANY
P.O. Box 3226, 1805 South Main Street, Seattle WA 98114. 206/322-4242. Contact Rod Falor, Personnel Director. A facility operating as part of the largest wholesale bakery operation in the United States, manufacturing and distributing a line of high quality bread and cake products. Parent company, Ralston Purina Company, is a major producer of consumer grocery products, livestock and pet food products, and other goods and services.

CONTINENTAL EMSCO COMPANY/ SKAGIT DIVISION
P.O. Box 151, 500 Metcalf, Sedro Woolley WA 98284. 206/855-1141. Contact Personnel Director. A manufacturer of heavy machinery such as cranes, logging equipment, and construction equipment.

CONTINENTAL VAN LINES, INC.
4501 West Marginal Way South West, Seattle WA 98106. 206/937-2261. Contact Personnel Department. A primary Seattle transportation company engaged in interstate moving and storage.

COONS, CORKER & ASSOCIATES
The Flour Mill, Penthouse Level, West 621 Mallon Avenue, Spokane WA 99201. 509/326-8310. Contact Personnel Manager. An area advertising agency offering advertising, marketing, and public relations. Common positions include: Accountant; Advertising Worker; Commercial Artist; Marketing Specialist; Public Relations Worker; Technical Writer/Editor; Copywriter; Account Executive. Principal educational

backgrounds sought: Art/Design; Communications; Marketing. Company benefits include: medical insurance; dental insurance.

CORROON & BLACK, INC.
2911 2nd Avenue, Seattle WA 98121. 206/443-2300. Contact Personnel Department. A principal Seattle insurance company engaged in commercial property, liability fidelity, security and life insurance, and group benefits.

CRAFTSMAN PRESS, INC.
1155 Valley Street, Seattle WA 98109. 206/682-8800. Contact Connie Nicholson, Personnel Director. A commercial printing firm.

THE CRESCENT
West 710 Riverside Avenue, Spokane WA 99201. 509/458-4124. Contact Kathryn Rigsby, Personnel Director. A major area full line, family-oriented department store offering a number of quality merchandise lines. Employs approximately 800 people. Common positions include: Advertising Worker, Buyer; Commercial Artist; Credit Manager; Customer Service Representative; Department Manager; Management Trainee; Personnel; Sales Representative; Merchandise Coordinator; Secretary. Principal educational backgrounds sought: Accounting; Art/Design; Business Administration; Liberal Arts; Communications. Company benefits include: medical insurance; dental insurance; life insurance; profit sharing; employee discounts; savings plan. Corporate and regional

headquarters location. Parent company: F&N Acquisition Corp.

CRESCENT MANUFACTURING COMPANY
25 South Hanford Street, P.O. Box 3985/98124, Seattle WA 98134. 206/623-7140. Contact Personnel Department. A prime manufacturing company dealing with mapleine raw and salted nuts, spices, extracts and seasoning mixes.

CRITON TECHNOLOGIES
10800 Northeast 8th Street, Suite 600, Bellevue WA 98004. 206/453-9400. Contact Ms. Huntley Holland, Director of Industrial Relations. A diversified manufacturer dealing in aerospace products, architectural products, and electronics and defense items. Eleven divisions are located in seven states; these divisions hire independently. Common positions include: Accountant; Blue-Collar Worker Supervisor; Buyer; Aerospace Engineer; Electrical Engineer; Industrial Engineer; Mechanical Engineer; Financial Analyst; Operations/Production Manager; Marketing Specialist; Personnel & Labor Relations Specialist; Quality Control Supervisor; Systems Analyst. Corporate headquarters location.

CURTICE BURNS FOODS
3303 South 35th Street, Tacoma WA 98409. 206/383-1621. Contact Personnel Department. A leading food manufacturing company specializing in mayonnaise, salad dressing, syrup, pickles, peppers, meats, entrees, and soups.

THE SEATTLE JOB BANK

CUSHMAN & WAKEFIELD OF WASHINGTON, INC.
999 Third Avenue, Suite 2600, Seattle WA 98104. 206/682-0666. Contact Susan Brookins, Personnel Director. An area real estate services firm offering sales, property management and appraisal services to a variety of clients.

CX CORPORATION
2700 Rainier Avenue South, Seattle WA 98144. 206/721-2233. Contact Personnel Department. A producer of a variety of electronic communications-related equipment and systems.

THE DAILY CHRONICLE
321 North Pearl, Centralia WA 98531. 206/736-3311. Contact Tom Ashton, Comptroller. Publishes a daily newspaper with a circulation of over 15,000.

THE DAILY NEWS
East 205 Main, Pullman WA 99163. 509/334-6397. Contact Managing Editor. Publishes an area newspaper. A member of the Tribune Publishing Company Group.

DAILY RECORD
4th & Main Street, P.O. Box 248, Ellensburg WA 98926. 509/925-1414. Contact John Ludtka, Editor/Publisher. The publisher of an area newspaper with a circulation of approximately 5,000.

THE DAILY WORLD
315 South Michigan, P.O. Box 269, Aberdeen WA 98520. 206/532-4000. Contact Duane Langliers, General Manager. Publishes a daily newspaper with a

circulation of over 15,000. A member of the Donrey Media Group.

DAIRY EXPORT COMPANY, INC.
635 Elliott Avenue West, Seattle WA 98119. 206/284-7220. Contact Personnel Department. A main Seattle company engaged in the manufacture and wholesale of animal feed and supplies.

DAIRYGOLD, INC.
635 Elliot Avenue West, Seattle WA 98119. 206/284-7220. Contact Karen White, Personnel Director. A company engaged in the production of a variety of dairy and animal food items for area customers. Employs over 900 people. Common positions include: Accountant; Attorney; Biologist; Blue-Collar Worker Supervisor; Computer Programmer; Credit Manager; Customer Service Representative; Industrial Engineer; Food Technologist; Sales Representative; Systems Analyst. Principal educational backgrounds sought: Accounting; Business Administration; Computer Science. Company benefits include: medical, dental and life insurance; pension plan; tuition assistance; disability coverage; savings plan. Corporate headquarters location.

DAISHOWA AMERICA COMPANY LTD.
7200 Columbia Center, Seattle WA 98104. 206/623-1772. Contact Personnel Department. A primary Seattle company engaged in the wholesale of wood chips.

DATA I/O CORPORATION

10525 Willows Road Northeast, P.O. Box 97046, Redmond WA 98073-9746. 206/881-6444. Contact Human Resources. A producer of electronics microprocessor based products and software. Employs over 400 people in the United States and abroad. Corporate headquarters location. Common positions include: Buyer; Electrical Engineer; Customer Service Representative; Financial Analyst; Technical Writer/Editor; Computer Programmer; Systems Analyst; Software Engineer. Principal educational backgrounds sought: Computer Science-Scientific Application only; Engineering-Electronics only; Communications; Marketing. Company benefits include: medical insurance; disability coverage; dental insurance; life insurance; tuition assistance; profit sharing; equal opportunity employer.

DATACOM NORTHWEST, INC.

11001 31st Place West, Everett WA 98204. 206/355-0590. Contact Valerie Herring, Personnel Director. A manufacturer of high-technology support equipment, digital test equipment, and related products.

DEL MONTE CORPORATION

P.O. Box 1528, Yakima WA 98907. 509/575-6580. Contact George Reed, Plant Manager. Nationally, the firm is a major processor and distributor of foods, operating in processed foods, fresh fruit, refrigerated transport operations, trucking, and institutional food services. This facility is engaged in the processing of canned fruits. Corporate headquarters location: San Francisco, CA. New York Stock Exchange.

DELOITTE HASKINS & SELLS
1111 Third Avenue, 11th Floor, Seattle WA 98101. 206/624-0050. Contact Personnel Manager. Nationally, the firm is a major certified public accounting firm providing professional accounting, auditing, tax, and management consulting services to widely diversified clients. Maintains more than 500 offices throughout the world; has specialized program consisting of some 25 national industry groups and 50 functional (technical) groups that cross industry lines. Groups are involved in various disciplines, including accounting and auditing, taxation, management advisory services, small and growing businesses, mergers and acquisitions, and computer applications. Corporate headquarters location: New York, NY.

DENNY'S RESTAURANTS
11411 Northeast, 124 Street, Suite 110, Kirkland WA 98034. 206/821-4640. Contact Mark Mueller, Regional Personnel Manager. A company engaged in the food service industry. Parent company operates two major restaurant chains: Denny's Restaurants, with over 900 outlets across the United States, and Winchell's Donut House, which maintains over 600 outlets, primarily in the western half of the country. Corporate headquarters location: La Mirada, CA. New York Stock Exchange.

DOWTY DECOTO, INC.
2720 West Washington Avenue, Yakima WA 98903. 509/248-5000. Contact Personnel Manager. A manufacturer of aerospace components and equipment. Corporate headquarters location. Operations at this

facility include: manufacturing; administration; sales. Common positions include: Bookkeeper; Buyer; Draftsperson; Hydraulic Assembler; Mechanical Engineer; Department Manager; Production Manager; Marketing Specialist; Production Control Specialist; Production Supervisor; Personnel & Labor Relations Specialist; Quality Inspector; Quality Assurance Supervisor. Company benefits include: medical insurance; dental insurance; pension plan; life insurance; tuition assistance; disability coverage; profit sharing.

DP ENTERPRISES, INC.
1300 Dexter Avenue North, Seattle WA 98109. 206/283-1300. Contact Personnel Department. A nationwide computer sales, leasing, service and support firm. Common job positions include: Accountant; Buyer; Department Manager; Marketing Specialist; Personnel & Labor Relations Specialist; Purchasing Agent; Sales Representative; Transportation & Traffic Specialist; Computer Support Services; Computer Repair Technician. Principal educational backgrounds sought: Accounting; Business Administration; Computer Science. Company benefits include: medical insurance; dental insurance; 401K; life insurance; tuition assistance; disability coverage; employee discounts. Corporate headquarters. Operations at this facility include: regional headquarters; administration; service; sales.

EAGLE MARINE SERVICES LTD.
3443 West Marginal Way South West, Seattle WA 98106. 206/292-4646. Contact Steve Doring, Personnel

Department. A principal Seattle company engaged in stevedoring, the loading and unloading of ships.

EDAW, INC.
121 First Avenue South, Seattle WA 98104. 206/622-1176. Contact Bryce Ecklaine, Principal in Charge. Provides landscape architecture, environmental planning and urban design services throughout the United States and in many foreign countries. Corporate headquarters: San Francisco, CA.

EGGHEAD, INC.
22011 South East 51st Street, Issaquah WA 98027. 206/391-0800. Contact Personnel Department. A major computer and software retailer.

EHRIG & ASSOCIATES
2615 Fourth Avenue Suite 800, Seattle WA 98121. 206/441-6666. Contact Personnel Department. A major Seattle advertising agency.

ELDEC CORPORATION
16700 13th Avenue West, Lynnwood WA 98036-0100. 206/743-8239. Contact Employment Department. A custom-designer and builder of precision electronic equipment for the aerospace industry. The corporation has four major operating groups: Power Conversion Division; Sensing Systems Division; Monitor and Control Division; and Transducers, Inc., a wholly-owned subsidiary. Corporate headquarters location. Operations at this facility include: manufacturing; research/development. Common positions include: Accountant; Buyer; Computer Programmer; Customer

Service Representative; Draftsperson; Electrical Engineer; Industrial Engineer; Mechanical Packaging Engineer; Test Engineer; Quality Control Engineer; Operations/Production Manager; Marketing Specialist; Personnel & Labor Relations Specialist; Physicist; Systems Analyst; Technical Writer/Editor. Principal educational backgrounds sought: Business Administration; Computer Science; Engineering; Physics. Company benefits include: medical insurance; dental insurance; pension plan; life insurance; tuition assistance; disability coverage; profit sharing; employee discounts; savings plan.

ELGEE CORPORATION
South 3021 Regal, Spokane WA 99223. 509/535-0631. Contact Personnel Department. A leading advertising agency.

ELGIN SYFERD
411 First Avenue South, Seattle WA 98104. 206/442-9900. Contact Personnel Department. A leading advertising agency.

ENGINEERING DEVELOPMENT CORPORATION
3400 South 150th Street, Seattle WA 98188. 206/243-7552. Contact Personnel Department. A prominent Seattle company engaged in the remanufacturing of diesel component parts.

EP INDUSTRIES, INC.
801 Houser Way North, Renton WA 98055. 206/235-8466. Contact Personnel Department. The retailer of

recreational sports equipment, also manufacture E.P. Vector recreational and performance water skis.

ESTERLINE CORPORATION
10800 North East 8th Street, Bellevue WA 98004. 206/453-6001. Contact Huntley Holland, Personnel Department. A corporation specializing in printed circuit board drilling machinery, production machinery for electronics & semiconductor industries.

EVANS/KRAFT, INC.
190 Queen Anne Avenue North, Seattle WA 98109-4924. 206/285-2222. Contact Personnel Director. An advertising agency offering a variety of services.

EVERYLIFE NUTRITIONALS, INC.
2021 15th Avenue West, Seattle WA 98119. 206/285-3800. Contact Personnel Department. A leading manufacturer of vitamins and OTC pharmaceuticals.

EXPEDITORS INTERNATIONAL OF WASHINGTON
19119 16th Avenue, Seattle WA 98188. 206/246-3711. Contact Personnel Department. A leading Seattle company engaged in freight forwarding and cargo transportation.

EZ LOADER BOAT TRAILERS, INC.
P.O. Box 3263TA, Spokane WA 99220. 509/489-0181. Contact Bill Baker, Personnel Director. A manufacturer of boat trailers.

THE SEATTLE JOB BANK

FACTORY MUTUAL ENGINEERING AND RESEARCH
10900 Northeast 8th Street, Suite 1105, Plaza Center Building, Bellevue WA 98004. 206/454-3931. Contact District Supervisor. A loss-prevention service organization maintained by the Factory Mutual System, with district offices located throughout the U.S. and Canada. The Loss Prevention Consultants inspect insured properties on a periodic basis to help pinpoint hazards or conditions that could cause fires or explosions and result in damage to property and lost production. During their inspections, they also determine that fire protection systems and equipment are adequate and in good condition. Corporate headquarters location: Norwood, MA.

FAMILY LIFE INSURANCE COMPANY
Park Place, 1200 Sixth Avenue, Seattle WA 98101. 206/292-1000. Contact Personnel Department. A prominent insurance agency, dealing mostly with mortgage protection, life and disability insurance, single premium, and whole life and annuities.

FAMILY SAVINGS AND LOAN ASSOCIATION
1107 North East 45th Street, Seattle WA 98145-0580. 206/547-6043. Contact Personnel Department. A primary Seattle savings and loan association.

FARMERS NEW WORLD LIFE INSURANCE COMPANY
3003 77th Avenue, Mercer Island WA 98040. 206/232-8400. Contact Gretchen Miller, Personnel Director. Offers a line of life insurance products, including group

life and medical coverages. A subsidiary of the Farmers Group Inc. Corporate headquarters location: Los Angeles, CA.

FARWEST SEAFOODS, INC.
North Tower, 100 West Harrison Plaza, Seattle WA 98109. 206/285-0300. Contact Personnel Department. A leading seafood company.

FEDERATED AMERICAN INSURANCE COMPANY
15300 Bothell Way North East, Seattle WA 98155. 206/364-3010. Contact Personnel Department. A primary Seattle insurance company specializing in auto insurance.

FENTRON BUILDING PRODUCTS, INC.
2801 Northwest Market Street, Seattle WA 98107. 206/782-2000. Contact Sales Manager. A manufacturer of a line of housing and decorative products, including metal doors, windows, and curtain accessories.

FIREMAN'S FUND INSURANCE COMPANY
2121 4th Avenue, Seattle WA 98121. 206/728-5252. Contact Shari Makamura, Human Resource Representative. A company which offers a variety of insurance products and services to area customers. Common positions include: Accountant; Administrator; Attorney; Claim Representative; Branch Manager; Operations/Production Manager; Marketing Specialist; Personnel & Labor Relations Specialist; Quality Control Supervisor; Underwriter. Principal educational backgrounds sought include: Accounting; Business Administration; Communications; Economics; Finance;

Liberal Arts; Marketing; Mathematics. Company benefits include: medical, dental and life insurance; pension plan; tuition assistance; disability coverage; employee discounts; savings plan. Corporate, divisional headquarters location: San Rafael, CA. Operations at this facility include: administration; service.

FIRESTONE TIRE & RUBBER COMPANY
19518 Pacific Highway South, Suite 101, Seattle WA 98188. 206/878-5434. Contact John Steinley, Personnel. A company primarily engaged in the development, manufacture, and sale of a broad line of tires for the original equipment and replacement markets of the world. Manages its business through three primary operating units: the World Tire Group is responsible for the design, development, testing, and manufacturing of tires throughout the world; the Sales and Marketing Group is a nationwide sales network which includes dealer outlets and automotive service centers; and the Corporate Development Group has the responsibility for corporate strategic planning activities. Corporate headquarters location: Akron, OH. New York Stock Exchange.

FIRST CITY CREDIT
600 Stewart Street, Seattle WA 98101. 206/621-5001. Contact Personnel Department. A leading Seattle company engaged in equipment rental and leasing.

FIRST CITY INVESTMENTS, INC.
800 5th Avenue Suite 4170, Seattle WA 98104. 206/624-9223. Contact Personnel Department. A principal real estate developer, lender.

FIRST INTERSTATE BANK OF WASHINGTON
999 Third Avenue, P.O. Box 160/98111, Seattle WA 98104. 206/292-3111. Contact Personnel Department. A primary Seattle bank.

FIRST NATIONAL INSURANCE CO. OF AMERICA
Safeco Plaza, Seattle WA 98185. 206/545-5000. Contact Personnel Department. A primary Seattle company engaged in property and casualty insurance.

FIRST REAL ESTATE SALES, INC.
8001 15th North West, Seattle WA 98117. 206/784-9811. Contact Personnel Department. A prominent real estate operators and agents company.

FISCHER DIAC DEVELOPMENT, INC.
937 Harvard Avenue East, Seattle WA 98102. 206/328-2000. Contact Personnel Department. A primary Seattle company engaged in real estate development.

FISHERIES SUPPLY COMPANY
1900 North Northlake Way, Seattle WA 98103. 206/632-4462. Contact Personnel Department. A key wholesaler of industrial hardware and supplies.

FLIGHTCRAFT
8285 Perimeter Road South, Boeing Field, Seattle WA 98108. 206/764-6100. Contact Rick Fenberg, Sales Department. A leading Northwestern general aviation company offering flight training, aviation sales and service, and air charter flights. Founded 1948. Other area facilities: Spokane, WA, Portland, OR.

JOHN FLUKE MANUFACTURING COMPANY, INC.
6920 Seaway Boulevard, P.O. Box C9090/98206, Everett WA 98203. 206/347-6100. Contact Personnel Department. A major eletrical manufacturer of electronic instrumentation, test measurement and calibration.

FOOD GIANT STORES
P.O. Box 31088, Seattle WA 98103. 206/632-9253. Contact Ken Gilman, Assistant General Manager. Operates a chain of food stores.

FOOD SERVICES OF AMERICA
18430 East Valley Highway, Seattle WA 98124. 206/251-1370. Contact Carol Sidell, Administative Services Manager. A food service company specializing in the distribution of Snoboy fruit and vegetables, FSA canned and frozen foods, beverages, serving equipment, cleaning supplies, tableware, paper products, "dry goods and fresh" fish. Common job positions include: Accountant; Administrator; Customer Service Representative; Department Manager; General Manager; Operations/Production Manager; Marketing Specialist; Personnel & Labor Relations Specialist; Purchasing Agent; Quality Control Supervisor; Sales Representative; Systems Analyst. Principal educational backgrounds sought: Accounting; Business Administration; Communications; Finance; Liberal Arts; Marketing; Wholesale Food. Company benefits include: medical insurance; dental insurance; pension plan; life insurance; tuition assistance; disability coverage; profit sharing; employee discounts; savings

plan. Corporate headquarters. Parent Company is Stevedoring Services of America. Operations at this facility include: service; sales.

FOSS LAUNCH & TUG COMPANY
660 West Ewing, Seattle WA 98119. 206/281-3800. Contact Personnel Department. A primary maritime carrier, deep-sea forum, domestic, coast-wise and intercoastal transportation, ship repair, and wholesaler of wire and rope.

FOSTER & MARSHALL/ AMERICAN EXPRESS, INC.
999 3rd Avenue, Seattle WA 98104. 206/344-3500. Contact Personnel Department. A prominent investment banker.

FOXS GEMSHOP, INC.
1341 5th Avenue, Seattle WA 98101. 206/441-3697. Contact Personnel Department. A key Seattle company engaged in the retail of jewelry.

FREMONT ELECTRIC COMPANY
744 North 34th, Seattle WA 98103. 206/633-2323. Contact Personnel Department. A prominent Seattle wholesaler and retailer for the automotive industry.

GACO WESTERN, INC.
P.O. Box 88698, Seattle WA 98138-2698. 206/575-0450. Contact Personnel Department. A leading Seattle manufacturer of elastomeric coatings.

GAI'S SEATTLE FRENCH BAKING COMPANY
P.O. Box 24327, 2006 South Weller Street, Seattle WA 98144. 206/329-3000. Contact Don Gai, General Manager & Vice-President. A producer of a variety of bakery products, including buns, breadsticks, pastries, and bread.

GAN ENTERPRISES, INC.
14900 Interurban Avenue S, Seattle WA 98168. 206/451-0790. Contact Personnel Department. A principal Seattle operative builder real estate agents company.

GEM EAST CORP.
2124 2nd Avenue, Seattle WA 98121. 206/441-1700. Contact Personnel Department. A main Seattle company engaged in the manufacture and wholesale of jewelry.

GENERAL BREWING CORPORATION
312 West 8th Street, Vancouver WA 98660. 206/695-3381. Contact Personnel Department. The brewing company for Lucky Lager, Lucky Draft, Fisher, Regal Beers.

GENERAL INSURANCE COMPANY OF AMERICA
Safeco Plaza, Seattle WA 98185. 206/545-5000. Contact Personnel Department. A major Seattle property and casualty insurance company.

GENERAL TELEPHONE COMPANY OF THE NORTHWEST

1800 41st, 3-HR, Everett WA 98201. 206/258-5688. Contact Cindi Philips, Employment Representative. A company providing telecommunications services to area customers. Employs over 5,000 people. Regional and divisional headquarters location. Operations at this facility include: administration; service; sales. Corporate headquarters location: Stamford, CT. Common positions include: Accountant; Administrator; Blue-Collar Worker Supervisor; Computer Programmer; Customer Service Representative; Draftsperson; Engineer; Electrical Engineer; Financial Analyst; Marketing Specialist; Programmer; Sales Representative; Statistician; Systems Analyst. Principal educational backgrounds sought: Accounting; Business Administration; Communications; Computer Science; Economics; Engineering; Finance; Liberal Arts; Marketing. Company benefits include: medical insurance; dental insurance; pension plan; life insurance; tuition assistance; disability coverage; employee discounts; savings plan.

GIBRALTAR SAVINGS OF WASHINGTON F.A.

11000 Northeast Thirty-Third Place, Bellview WA 98004. 206/828-0404. Contact Peter Rumwell, Personnel Director. A major area savings and loan institution. Parent company: Gibraltar Financial Corporation, a diversified financial services company with operations in securities, insurance, leasing, and many other areas. Corporate headquarters location: Beverly Hills, CA.

THE SEATTLE JOB BANK

GLACIER PARK COMPANY
1011 Western Avenue, Seattle WA 98101. 206/625-6300. Contact Personnel Department. A primary Seattle real estate leasor and developer.

GM NAMEPLATE, INC.
2040 15th Avenue West, Seattle WA 98119. 206/284-2200. Contact Personnel Department. A prime Seattle company involved in coating, engraving, allied services, paper coatings, glazing.

GOLUB SIMON & SONS, INC.
5506 6th Avenue, Seattle WA 98101. 206/762-4800. Contact Personnel Department. A prominent Seattle company engaged in the wholesale and manufacture of jewelry, watches, and precious metals.

JOHN GRAHAM & COMPANY
520 Pike Street, Suite 1100, Seattle WA 98101. 206/447-5600. Contact Jim Pearce, Personnel Director. A company offering a wide range of planning and design services, primarily for projects in the Pacific Northwest. Also offers specialized consulting services. Corporate headquarters location.

GRANGE INSURANCE
200 Cedar Street, Seattle WA 98121. 206/448-4911. Contact Personnel Department. A primary insurance underwriting company of Seattle.

GRAYS HARBOR DIVISION/ ITT RAYONIER
23rd & Railroad, P.O. Box 299, Hoquiam WA 98550. 206/532-1410. Contact Clyde Stevenson, Personnel Director. A producer of chemical fibers and pulp products for a variety of end uses. Employs over 600 people.

GREAT REPUBLIC LIFE INSURANCE
226 2nd Avenue West, Seattle WA 98119. 206/285-1422. Contact Personnel Department. A main Seattle health insurance underwriting company.

GREAT WESTERN FEDERAL SAVINGS BANK
11201 Southeast 8th Street, Bellevue WA 98004. Mailed inquiries only. Contact Cheryl McDonald, Personnel Director. An area financial institution with strong emphasis on mortgage banking. Corporate headquarters location. Operations at this facility include: research/development; administration; service; sales. American Stock Exchange. Common positions include: Accountant; Administrator; Bank Officer/Manager; Computer Programmer; Customer Service Representative; Branch Manager; Marketing Specialist; Personnel and Labor Relations Specialist; Purchasing Agent; Systems Analyst; Underwriter; Teller; Secretary. Principal educational backgrounds sought: Accounting; Business Administration; Computer Science; Economics; Finance. Company benefits include: medical insurance; dental insurance; pension plan; life insurance; tuition assistance; disability coverage; profit sharing.

GREEN GIANT COMPANY/DAYTON PLANT
711 East Main, P.O. Box 26, Dayton WA 99328. 509/382-2511. Contact Duane Dunlap, Personnel Director. A major area producer of canned food products, including asparagus. A division of Pillsbury Company. Corporate headquarters location: Minneapolis, MN.

GREENWOOD ENTERPRISES
409 Roy Street Suite 208, Seattle WA 98108. 206/282-8998. Contact Personnel Department. A primary Seattle company that owns, operates, and leases property.

H&N, INC.
15305 Northeast 40th Street, Redmond WA 98052. 206/885-1414. Contact Kay Pike, Personnel Director. A poultry producer maintaining breeding and related operations.

HAGGEN COMPANY
P.O. Box 489, Bellingham WA 98227. 206/733-8720. Contact Personnel Director. Engaged in grocery item and greeting card operations.

HEATH TECNA AEROSPACE COMPANY
19819 84th Avenue South, Kent WA 98032. 206/872-7500. Contact Mr. Hedman, Director of Industrial Relations. A producer of composite, metal, fiberglass and plastic aircraft components for use in commercial jet airliners and other aerospace applications. Employs over 800 people.

HEMPHILL BROTHERS, INC.
P.O. Box 80786, Seattle WA 98108. 206/762-7622. Contact Personnel Department. A prime Seattle manufacturer of crushed limestone and silica sand.

THE HERALD
P.O. Box 930, Everett WA 98206. 206/339-3456. Contact Human Resources Department. Publishes a daily newspaper, with an approximate circulation of 57,000. Part of the Washington Post Newspaper Group (Washington, DC). Divisional headquarters location. Operations at this facility include: manufacturing;research/development; administration; sales. Corporate headquarters location: Washington, DC. Common positions include: Accountant; Administrator; Advertising Worker; Blue-Collar Worker Supervisor; Commercial Artist; Computer Programmer; Credit Manager; Customer Service Representative; Financial Analyst; Department Manager; Operations/Production Manager; Personnel & Labor Relations Specialist; Purchasing Agent; Reporter/Editor; Sales Representative; Systems Analyst; Technical Writer/Editor; Transportation & Traffic Specialist. Principal educational backgrounds sought: Accounting; Art/Design; Business Administration; Communications; Finance; Liberal Arts; Marketing; Journalism. Company benefits include: medical insurance; dental insurance; life insurance; tuition assistance; disability coverage; profit sharing; employee discounts; savings plan.

HEWLETT-PACKARD COMPANY
P.O. Box C-006, Vancouver WA 98668. 206/254-8110. Contact Artis Vidan, Personnel Director. Nationally, company is a worldwide firm engaged in the design, manufacture, marketing, and servicing of a broad array of precision electronics instruments and systems for analysis, measurement, and computation. Company's line of over 6,000 products is used in business, industry, engineering, science, education, and medicine. The company employs approximately 82,000 people in 23 U.S. cities and around the world. Corporate headquarters location: Palo Alto, CA. New York Stock Exchange.

HOAGY'S CORNER RESTAURANTS
1035 Andover Parkway West, Tukwila WA 98188. 206/575-0107. Contact Personnel Department. The operator of Hoagy's Corner fast food restaurant/convenience stores.

HOLLAND AMERICA LINE WESTOURS
300 Elliott Avenue West, Seattle WA 98119. 206/281-3535. Contact Personnel Department. A leading tour and cruise operator.

HONEYWELL, INC./
MARINE SYSTEMS DIVISION
6500 Harbor Heights Parkway, Everett WA 98204. 206/789-2000. Contact Personnel Director. A manufacturer of naval sonar and acoustic equipment for offshore oil and commercial marine applications. Nationally, company is a high technology firm doing business in four industry segments: Aerospace and

Defense, Control Products, Control Systems, and Information Systems. Corporate headquarters location: Minneapolis, MN. New York Stock Exchange.

HORIZON AIR INDUSTRIES, INC.
19521 Pacific Highway S., P.O. Box 48309, Seattle WA 98198. 206/241-6757. Contact Personnel Department. A prominent passenger freight company in Seattle.

HYGRADE FOOD PRODUCTS CORPORATION
P.O. Box 1636, Tacoma WA 98401. 206/627-8121. Contact Personnel Director. A producer of meat products, including sausage, smoked meats, and canned ham. Employs over 500 people.

IBM CORPORATION
One Union Square, Suite 101, 600 University, Seattle WA 98101. 206/587-3190. Contact IBM Central Employment Office. Nationally, the firm is a major worldwide manufacturer and supplier in the area of information technology. Products include data processing machines and systems, telecommunications systems and products, information distributors, office systems, typewriters, copiers, educational and testing materials, and related supplies and services. Operates worldwide through the following groups, each comprised of several operating divisions: Information Systems Group; Information Systems And Technology Group; and Information Systems and Communications Group. Subsidiaries include: IBM Credit Corporation; IBM Instruments, Inc.; and IBM World Trade Corporation. Corporate headquarters location: Armonk, NY. New York Stock Exchange.

ICICLE SEAFOODS, INC.
4019 21st Avenue West, P.O. Box 79003, Seattle WA 98119. 206/282-0988. Contact Personnel Department. A principal Seattle seafood company engaged in the manufacture of canned and frozen fish, shellfish, and shrimp based products.

IGM COMMUNICATIONS
4041 Home Road, Bellingham WA 98226. 206/733-4567. Contact Rick Sawyer, Operations Manager. An electronics company manufacturing instacart and go-cart random access and audio cartridge handling systems along with computer based automation systems.

IMAGES WOODWORKING, INC.
1601 One Union Square, Seattle WA 98101. 206/621-8884. Contact Personnel Department. A major woodworking company.

IMMUNEX CORPORATION
51 University Street, Seattle WA 98101. 206/587-0430. Contact Human Resources Department. A Seattle biotechnology company, researching and developing pharmaceutical products. Common job positions include: Biochemist; Biologist; Research Assistant. Principal educational backgrounds sought: Biology;

Chemistry; Immunology. Company benefits include: medical insurance; dental insurance; pension plan; life insurance; disability coverage; stock options; transportation assistance. Corporate headquarters. Operations at this facility include: manufacturing; research/development; administration.

IMRE CORPORATION
130 Fifth Avenue, North, Seattle WA 98109. 206/448-1000. Contact Personnel Department. A major manufacturer of medical products.

INCO EXPRESS, INC.
3600 South 124th, Seattle WA 98168. 206/248-2700. Contact Personnel Department. A primary long distance trucking company.

INTALCO ALUMINUM CORPORATION
P.O. Box 937, Ferndale WA 98248. 206/384-7061. Contact Sally Thorinson, Personnel Supervisor. Primary aluminum manufacturing plant. Parent company: Alumax, Inc. Common positions include: Electrical Engineer; Industrial Engineer; Mechanical Engineer; Metallurgical Engineer. Principal educational background sought: Engineering. Company benefits include: medical, dental, and life insurance; pension plan; tuition assistance; disability coverage; profit sharing; savings plan. Corporate headquarters location: San Mateo, CA.

INTEGRATED CIRCUITS, INC.
10301 Willows Road, Redmond WA 98052. 206/882-3100. Contact Greg Guetzlec, Human Resources

Administrator. A manufacturer of electronic circuit equipment including microcircuits and dc/dc power converters. Common positons include: Draftsperson; Electrical Engineer. Principal educational backgrounds sought include: Engineering. Company benefits include: medical, dental and life insurance; tuition assistance; disability coverage; profit sharing.

INTERMEC CORPORATION
4405 Russell Road, P.O. Box 360602, Lynnwood WA 98046-9702. 206/348-2600. Contact Personnel Department. An equipment manufacturer of Bar Code (computer peripheral, products).

INTERPACIFIC INVESTORS SERVICES
801 2nd Avenue Suite 612, Seattle WA 98104. 206/623-2784. Contact Personnel Department. A prominent Seattle mutual funds and life insurance brokerage firm, also dealing with corporation and municipal bonds.

INTERSTATE DISTRIBUTOR COMPANY
P.O. Box 99909, Tacoma WA 98499. Mailed inquiries only. Contact George Payne, Vice President/Finance. A companye engaged in trucking and related transport activities. Common positions include: Accountant; Claim Representative; Computer Programmer; Dispatcher; Credit Manager; Branch Manager; Department Manager; General Manager; Operations/Production Manager; Personnel & Labor Relations Specialist; Sales Representative; Transportation & Traffic Specialist. Principal educational backgrounds sought: Accounting; Computer Science. Company benefits include: medical, dental, and

life insurance; tuition assistance; profit sharing. Corporate headquarters location. Operations at this facility include: administration; service; sales.

JAY JACOBS, INC.
1530 5th Avenue, Seattle WA 98101. 206/622-5400. Contact Personnel Department. A company engaged in the retailing of women and young mens clothing.

JAMES RIVER CORPORATION
P.O. Box 271, Port Angeles WA 98362. 206/457-4474. Contact Ted Weitman, Personnel Director. Mill facility of one of the nation's major paper manufacturers. Nationally, the firm is engaged in the manufacture and distribution of a broad and diversified product line including pulp, paper, logs, lumber, flexible packaging, and other items. This facility produces newsprint, pulp, and related items. Corporate headquarters location: San Francisco, CA. New York Stock Exchange.

JANTZEN, INC.
206 South Grand Boulevard, Vancouver WA 98661. 206/690-1300. Contact Jan Ronzheimer, Personnel Supervisor. A producer of women's swimwear and related apparel items for national distribution. Employs approximately 400 people.

JENSEN-BYRD COMPANY, INC.
310-324 West Riverside Avenue, Spokane WA 99201. 509/624-1321. Contact Personnel Coordinator. A wholesale distributor of hardware goods.

JAMES PAUL JONES
2634 Thorndyke Avenue West, Seattle WA 98199. 206/283-3012. Contact Personnel Department. A principal condo and non residential building construction and sales company.

JORGENSEN STEEL/ FORGE DIVISION
P.O. Box 24026, Seattle WA 98124. 206/762-1100. Contact Ron Altier, Personnel Director. A major producer of steel and related metals goods; the firm also provides customers with many additional services including sawing, flame cutting, grinding, and heat treating of metals. Corporate headquarters location: Lynnwood, CA. New York Stock Exchange.

JOURNAL-AMERICAN
P.O. Box 90130, Bellevue WA 98009-0130. 206/455-2222. Contact Curtis Uno, Vice-President/Employee Relations. Publishes a daily area newspaper with a circulation of approximately 28,000. A member of the McClelland Newspapers group.

K-MART STORES
130 and Aurora Avenue North, Seattle WA 98133. 206/363-6319. Contact Personnel Director. Nationally, the firm is one of the largest general-merchandise retailers in the world. The firm operates 2,400 retail stores in the United States, Canada, and Puerto Rico, under such trade names as K-Mart, Kresge, and Jupiter. Corporate headquarters location: Troy, MI. New York Stock Exchange. Company benefits include: medical

insurance; pension plan; life insurance; disability coverage; savings plan.

K2 CORPORATION
19215 99th Avenue Southwest, Vashon WA 98070. 206/463-3631. Contact Charlie Jenkins, Personnel Director. A major producer of camping and skiing equipment, including tents, skis, and bondings. Employs over 800 people. Corporate headquarters location. Common positions include: Accountant; Buyer; Chemist; Computer Programmer; Credit Manager; Customer Service Representative; Chemical Engineer; Industrial Engineer; Mechanical Engineer; Department Manager; Operations/Production Manager; Purchasing Agent; Quality Control Supervisor; Systems Analyst. Principal educational backgrounds sought: Accounting; Business Administration; Engineering; Marketing. Company benefits include: medical insurance; dental insurance; life insurance; tuition assistance; disability coverage; employee discounts; savings plan.

KAISER ALUMINUM & CHEMICAL CORPORATION/
TRENTWOOD ROLLING MILL
P.O. Box 15108, Spokane WA 99215. 509/924-1500. Contact Personnel Director. A manufacturer of aluminum plate, sheet, and coil products for a variety of end uses. Employs more than 2,000 persons. Corporate headquarters location: Oakland, CA.

THE SEATTLE JOB BANK

KAVILCO, INC.
600 University Street, Seattle WA 98101. 206/624-6166. Contact Personnel Department. A company engaged in processing timber tracks and sawmills.

KENWORTH TRUCK COMPANY
P.O. Box 1000, 10630 Northeast 38th Place, Kirkland WA 98033. 206/828-5000. Contact Paul Poyfair, Personnel Director. A company which manufacturers trucks, a division of PACCAR, Inc. Employs over 1,000 people. Corporate headquarters location: Bellevue, WA.

HENRY H. KETCHAM LUMBER COMPANY, INC.
P.O. Box 22789, Seattle WA 98122. 206/329-2700. Contact Personnel Department. A leading wholesale lumber company.

KEY BANK OF PUGET SOUND
1536 North West Market Street, Seattle WA 98107. 206/789-4000. Contact Personnel Department. A prominent bank holding company.

KEY INDUSTRIES, INC.
2744 16th Avenue South West, Seattle WA 98129. 206/682-8700. Contact Personnel Department. A prominent wholesaler of industry supplies and commercial machines and equipment.

KEY TRONIC CORPORATION
P.O. Box 14687, Spokane WA 99214. 509/928-8000. Contact Personnel Director. A producer of equipment

and peripherals for use in computer systems, including keyboards and circuit boards. Employs over 900 people.

KIEWITT INDUSTRIAL COMPANY
P.O. Box 70, Anacortes WA 98221. 206/293-5180. Contact Buz Paulson, Construction Manager. Company engaged in the production of facilities for offshore energy development in the Pacific Northwest. Employs approximately 340 people.

KINNEAR OF WASHINGTON
2001 Industrial Drive, Centralia WA 98531. 206/736-7654. Contact Richard Rowan, Personnel Director. A manufacturer of garage doors and related wood items. A division of Hardsco Corporation. Corporate headquarters location: Camp Hill, PA.

KNIK CONSTRUCTION COMPANY, INC.
P.O. Box 3757, Seattle WA 98124-3757. 206/241-8778. Contact Personnel Department. A prominent construction company of Seattle with numerous responsibilities as asphalt paving, airport construction, grading crushed rock, sand and gravel operations, earth moving, excavation and hauling.

KORRY ELECTRONICS
901 Dexter Avenue North, Seattle WA 98109. Mailed inquiries only. Contact Personnel Department. A manufacturer of electronic switching equipment and related products.

LAKE STEVENS INSTRUMENT DIVISION
HEWLETT PACKARD

8600 Soper Hill Road, Everett WA 98205-1298. Mailed inquiries only. Contact Staffing Department. A producer of synthesizers and low-frequency spectrum and network analyzers for communications and electronics equipment; waveform generators and dynamics analyzers for electromechanical and mechanical systems. Parent company, Hewlett Packard, is engaged in the design and manufacture of measurement and computation products and systems used in business, industry, engineering, science, health care, and education; principal products are integrated instrument and computer systems (including hardware and software), computer systems and peripheral products, and medical electronic equipment and systems. Common positions include: Electrical Engineer; Financial Analyst. Principal educational backgrounds sought: Computer Science; Economics; Finance; Software Engineer (ee/cs). Corporate headquarters location: Palo Alto, CA. Operations at this facility include: manufacturing; research/development.

LANGENDORF BAKING COMPANY
OF SEATTLE, INC.

P.O. Box 3664, 2901 6th Avenue South, Seattle WA 98124. 206/682-2244. Contact Beverly Glober, Office Manager. A producer of bread, pastry, and other bakery products. Employs approximately 340 people.

LANOGA COROPORATION

P.O. Box 97040, 17946 Northeast 65th, Redmond WA 98073. 206/883-4125. Contact Human Resources. A retailer of building materials to both contractor and consumer customers. Located in eleven midwestern and western states and Alaska. 1985 sales of approximately $400 million. Corporate headquarters location. Common positions include: Accountant; Administrator; Advertising Worker; Customer Service Representative; Draftsperson; Financial Analyst; General Manager; Management Trainee; Marketing Specialist; Personnel & Labor Relations Specialist; Sales Representative. Principal educational backgrounds sought: Accounting; Business Administration; Engineering; Marketing; Sales; Construction Engineering. Company benefits include: medical insurance; dental insurance; pension plan; life insurance; tuition assistance; disability coverage; profit sharing; employee discounts.

PALMER G. LEWIS COMPANY, INC.

525 C Street Northwest, Auburn WA 98001. 206/941-2600. Contact Director/Employee Relations. A wholesale distributor of building materials. Primary customers include retail building material dealers. Corporate, regional and divisional headquarters location. Common positions include: Accountant; Buyer; Computer Programmer; Credit Manager; Financial Analyst; Branch Manager; Department Manager; Management Trainee; Marketing Specialist; Purchasing Agent; Sales Representative. Principal educational backgrounds sought: Accounting; Business Administration; Communications; Economics; Finance; Marketing. Company benefits include: medical

insurance; dental insurance; life insurance; disability coverage; profit sharing; savings plan. Operations at this facility include: adminstration; sales.

LIBERTY ORCHARDS COMPANY, INC.
117-123 Mission, P.O. Box C, Cashmere WA 98815. 509/782-2191. Contact Personnel Department. An orchard specializing in the production of aplets, cotlets, grapelets, fruit and nut candies, fruit festives, fruit and nut candies.

LINDAL CEDAR HOMES, INC.
4300 South 104th Place, Seattle WA 98124. 206/725-0900. Contact Personnel Department. A prime manufacturer of pre-cut cedar homes and wholesalers of lumber and other building materials.

LIVINGSTON & COMPANY
800 Fifth Avenue Suite 3800, Seattle WA 98104. 206/382-5500. Contact Personnel Department. A premier Seattle advetising agency.

LONGVIEW FIBRE COMPANY
P.O. Box 639, Longview WA 98632. 206/425-1550. Contact Mr. Lou Metzler, Personnel Director. A company producing a variety of paper goods for industry and business, including bags and corrugated shipping containers.

LYDEN, INC.
18000 Pacific Highway South Suite 800, Seattle WA 98188. 206/241-8778. Contact Personnel Department.

A key holding company for transportation and construction industries.

MAC PHERSONS, INC.
5201 University Way, Seattle WA 98105. 206/525-6300. Contact Personnel Department. A principal realtor company of Seattle.

MAC-RENT, INC.
5201 University Way North East, Seattle WA 98105. 206/364-9977. Contact Personnel Department. A prominent company of Seattle with numerous responsibilies such as a holding company, real estate agents, developers; and apartment building operators.

MADRONA PUBLISHERS, INC.
P.O. Box 22667, Seattle WA 98122. 206/325-3973. Contact Sara Levant, Managing Editor. An area publishing firm, founded 1974.

MAGNOLIA HI-FI, INC.
3701 7th Avenue South, Seattle WA 98134. 206/623-7872. Contact Personnel Department. A primary retailer of stereophonic video equipment and car stereos.

MANAGEMENT AND PLANNING SERVICES
111 South Jackson, Seattle WA 98104. 206/223-5100. Contact Pola Piper, Office Manager. A company providing physical planning services, urban design, economic planning, and consulting services for a variety of clients. Parent company: The NBBJ Group (Seattle, WA).

MANKE LUMBER COMPANY, INC.
1717 Marine View Drive, Tacoma WA 98422. 206/572-6252. Contact Personnel Director. A manufacturer of a variety of lumber products, including wood chips and building materials.

MANNESMANN TALLY CORPORATION
8301 South 180th Street, Kent WA 98032. 206/251-5500. Contact Personnel Department. A major corporation dealing with laser, serial and line matrix printers, data communication systems, and teleprinters.

MANSON CONSTRUCTION ENGINEERING COMPANY
5209 East Marginal Way, P.O. Box 24067, Seattle WA 98124. 206/762-0850. Contact Personnel Department. A principal Seattle construction company engaged in general highway and street repair and other heavy construction.

MANUFACTURERS HANOVER
10740 Meridian Avenue North, Seattle WA 98133. 206/362-4566. Contact Manager. A company providing a broad range of financial services to area customers. Parent company: Manufacturers Hanover Corporation, a major national financial services company with operations in consumer banking, correspondent banking, and investment services. Corporate headquarters location: New York, NY.

MARCO SEATTLE
2300 West Commodore Way, Seattle WA 98199. 206/285-3200. Contact Hank Schlapp, Personnel Director. A manufacturer of commercial marine machinery, and fishing gear, equipment and vessels. Other operations include oil-spill management systems and related pollution control items. Employs over 600 people.

MARINE POWER & EQUIPMENT COMPANY, INC.
1441 North Northlake Way, Seattle WA 98103. 206/632-1441. Contact Ms. Cole, Personnel Director. A company engaged in the building and repairing of a variety of ships. Employs over 450 people.

MARKET FINANCE COMPANY
3301 South Norfolk, P.O. Box 3763, Seattle WA 98124. 206/762-2100. Contact Personnel Department. A prominent Seattle company engaged in short-term credit and equipment leasing.

MARSH & McLENNAN
720 Olive Way, Seattle WA 98101. 206/223-1240. Contact Lois Struthers, Personnel. A company which provides a wide variety of insurance products and services to area customers.

MASON PROPERTIES
1100 9th Avenue, P.O. Box 900/98111, Seattle WA 98101. 206/223-6600. Contact Personnel Department. A prime non-residential building operator of Seattle.

MAYR BROTHERS LOGGING COMPANY, INC.
Route 3, P.O. Box 180, Hoquiam WA 98550. 206/532-7490. Contact Personnel Director. An area logging firm with operations in wood chips and related forest products.

McCANN-ERICKSON/SEATTLE
1011 Weston Avenue, Suite 600, Seattle WA 98104. 206/682-6360. Contact Betty Stack, Financial Administrator. An area advertising firm offering a variety of services. Corporate headquarters location: New York, NY.

MEHRER DRYWALL, INC.
2657 20th Avenue West, Seattle WA 98199. 206/282-4288. Contact Personnel Department. A prominent Seattle company engaged in drywall contracting.

MERLINO'S MACARONI, INC.
P.O. Box 1508, Kent WA 98035-1508. 206/872-7155. Contact Personnel Department. A corporation involved in the manufacturing and distribution of macaroni.

MERRILL & RING, INC.
1411 4th Avenue Building, Seattle WA 98101. 206/682-3939. Contact Personnel Department. A principal Seattle company engaged in the manufacturing of lumber and logging.

THE SEATTLE JOB BANK

METROPOLITAN FEDERAL SAVINGS & LOAN ASSOCIATION
1100 Olive Way, Seattle WA 98101. 206/625-1818. Contact Personnel Department. A leading savings and loan association.

MICROSOFT CORPORATION
16011 Northeast 36th Way, Box 97017, Redmond WA 98073-9717. 206/882-8080. Contact Human Resources. A company that designs, develops, markets and supports a product line of systems and applications microcomputer software for business and professional use.

MILLIMAN & ROBERTSON, INC.
1301 5th Avenue, Suite 3600, Seattle WA 98101. 206/624-7940. Contact Personnel Department. A leading nationwide actuarial services company. Common job positions include: Actuary. Principal eduational backgrounds sought: Computer Science; Mathematics. Company benefits include: medical insurance; pension plan; life insurance; profit sharing; savings plan. Corporate headquarters. Operations at this facility include: National headquarters; administration; service.

MOBIL OIL CORPORATION
P.O. Box 8, Ferndale WA 98248. 206/384-1011. Contact Mr. J.R. Eklund, Personnel Director. An area refiner of petroleum and related products including jet fuel, gasoline, and heating products. Nationally, the firm is engaged in petroleum and chemical products marketing, refining, manufacturing, exploration and

production, transportation, and research and development. Corporate headquarters location: New York, NY.

MODULINE INTERNATIONAL, INC.
P.O. Box 3000, Lacey WA 98503. 206/491-1130. Contact Personnel Director. A manufacturer of wooden storage and shelving products for a variety of applications.

MOGELGAARD AND ASSOCIATES
2025 1st Avenue Suite 600, Seattle WA 98121. 206/448-6303. Contact David Prindle, Office Manager. A major Seattle advertising agency. Common job positions include: Advertising Worker. Principal educational backgrounds sought: Art/Design; Liberal Arts. Company benefits include: medical insurance; dental insurance; pension plan; profit sharing. Corporate headquarters. Operations at this facility include: regional headquarters; divisional headquarters; research/development; administration; service; sales.

MOUNTAINEERS BOOKS
306 2nd Avenue West, Seattle WA 98119. 206/285-2665. Contact Donna De Shazo, Manager. An area publisher specializing in books relating to the outdoors, including maps and guidebooks.

LANCE MUELLER & ASSOCIATES
130 Lakeside, Seattle WA 98122. 206/325-2553. Contact Personnel Department. A premier Seattle architect commercial project company.

THE SEATTLE JOB BANK

MURRAY CHRISCRAFT WEST
P.O. Box 1095, Bellingham WA 98227. 206/676-6200. Contact Darrell Markwood, Personnel Manager. A producer of fiberglass boats and related items; employs approximately 500 people.

MUZAK
915 Yale Avenue, Seattle WA 98109. 206/682-3737. Contact Personnel Department. A company which provides satellite deliverence and on premises music services to commercial and retail establishments directly and through franchised dealers in the U.S. and internationally.

MWK INTERNATIONAL LTD, INC.
3214 16th Avenue SW, Seattle WA 98124. 206/682-2501. Contact Personnel Department. A key general overseas power plant construction and general contractor of industrial buildings and warehouses.

NACO-WEST, INC.
P.O. Box 1888, 12301 Northeast Tenth Place, Bellevue WA 98009. 206/455-3155. Contact Tita Jones, Personnel Director. A company which provides camping memberships and related services to area customers.

NALLEY'S FINE FOODS
P.O. Box 11046, Tacoma WA 98411. 206/383-1621. Contact Kent Roberts, Director of Personnel. A producer of a wide range of snack foods, including chips, dressings, pickles, and canned meats. A division of Curtice-Burns, Inc. Employs over 700 people.

NATIONAL MERIT INSURANCE COMPANY
P.O. Box 55369, Seattle WA 98155. 206/367-4888. Contact Personnel Department. A principal Seattle property and casualty insurance company.

THE NBBJ GROUP
111 South Jackson, Seattle WA 98104. 206/223-5555. Contact Personnel Director. A professional architectural planning and consulting organization with operations in a variety of areas. Corporate headquarters location.

NCR CORPORATION
15400 Southeast 30th Place, Bellevue WA 98007. 206/643-4150. Contact Al Horn, Administrative Manager. Nationally, the company develops, manufactures, markets, installs, and services business information processing systems for worldwide markets. Products include general-purpose computer systems, industry-specific occupational workstations, and computer components and equipment. Corporate headquarters location: Dayton, OH. New York Stock Exchange.

NEWS-TRIBUNE & LEDGER
P.O. Box 11000, 1950 South State Street, Tacoma WA 98411. 206/597-8511. Contact Jack Wilson, Human Resources Director. The publisher of an area newspaper with a circulation of over 100,000.

THE NEWTON COMPANY
255 Central Building, Seattle WA 98104. 206/623-1942. Contact Lillian Short, Assistant to President. A leading income property investment firm. Common job positions include: Financial Analyst; President and CEO; Real Estate Broker; Secretary/Bookkeeper. Principal educational backgrounds sought: Business Administration; Economics; Finance; Marketing. Operations at this facility include: Service.

NEYHART COMPANY
315 Seneca, Seattle WA 98101. 206/623-5110. Contact Personnel Department. A prominent Seattle apartment buildings operator.

NINTENDO OF AMERICA
4820 150th Avenue, North East, P.O. Box 957, Redmond WA 98052. 206/882-2040. Contact Personnel Department. A major importer, wholesaler, and manufacturer of electronic games, home video systems, games and watches.

NORDSTROM, INC.
1501 5th Avenue, Seattle WA 98101. 206/628-2111. Contact Personnel Department. A primary Seattle retailer of childrens, mens, and womens apparel and accessories, and shoe department stores.

NORTH STAR ICE EQUIPMENT CORPORATION
4511 Shilshole Avenue, North West, P.O. Box 70668, Seattle WA 98107. 206/784-4500. Contact Personnel Department. A manufacturer of continuous flake ice makers and mechanical ice dispensing systems.

NORTHERN AIR FREIGHT, INC.
320-120th Avenue, North East, P.O. Box 6969, Bellevue WA 98005. 206/646-7171. Contact Personnel Department. A major air freight forwarding company.

NORTHERN LIFE INSURANCE COMPANY
1110 3rd Avenue, Seattle WA 98111. 206/292-1111. Contact Personnel Department. A premier life insurance company.

NORTHGATE CENTERS
Northgate Shopping Center, 555 Northgate Mall Suite 210, Seattle WA 98124. 206/362-4777. Contact Personnel Department. A primary real estate holding company.

NORTHLAND CABLE PROPERTIES FOUR LTD.
1201 3rd Avenue Suite 3600, Seattle WA 98101. 206/621-1351. Contact Personnel Department. A prime Seattle cablevision service.

NORTHWEST BANK
1536 NW Market, Seattle WA 98107. 206/789-4000. Contact Personnel Department. A primary Seattle bank.

NORTHWEST DAIRYMENS ASSOCIATION
635 Elliott Avenue West, P.O. Box 79007, Seattle WA 98119. 206/284-8120. Contact Personnel Department. A prominent dairy company specializing in the processing of fluid milk, the manufacture of ice cream, condensed milk, evaporated milk, cheese, and butter.

NORTHWEST FISHERIES ASSOCIATION
2208 North West Market Street, Suite 311, Seattle WA 98107. 206/345-4593. Contact Personnel Department. A leading Seattle trade association.

NORTHWEST PROTECTIVE SERVICE, INC.
2700 Elliott Avenue, Seattle WA 98121. 206/448-4040. Contact Ken M. Nasworthy, Personnel Manager. A company providing security guard service for various clients, primarily banks, office buildings, and other customers. Company benefits include: medical insurance; life insurance; disability coverage; free uniforms and training.

NORTHWEST TIMBER DIVISION/ ITT RAYONIER
P.O. Box 539, Hoquiam WA 98550. 206/532-2500. Contact Personnel Director. A manufacturer of lumber products.

NORTHWESTERN DRUG COMPANY
801 "C" Street Northwest, Auburn WA 98002. 206/939-5550. Contact Rod Rhodes, Personnel Director. A company primarily engaged in the distribution of pharmaceutical products to medical facilities and retail drug outlets.

NORTHWESTERN GLASS
5801 East Marginal Way South, Seattle WA 98134. 206/762-0660. Contact John Anderson, Personnel Director. A producer of container products, including jars and bottles.

OLD NATIONAL BANCORP
428 Riverside, Spokane WA 99201. 509/456-2188. Contact Senior V.P./Human Resources. An area financial institution offering a wide range of financial services to its customers.

OLD STONE BANK OF WASHINGTON
P.O. Box 96025, Bellevue WA 98009-9625. 206/447-6404. Contact Personnel Director. A company offering a wide variety of financial services to area customers.

OLD STONE CAPITAL CORPORATION
P.O. Box 1770, Seattle WA 98111. 206/646-2900. Contact Personnel Department. A principal Seattle business investment company.

OLIN DEFENSE SYSTEMS GROUP
11441 Willows Road, Redmond WA 98052. 206/885-5000. Contact John Knapp, Employment Manager. A division of a major corporation engaged in manufacturing of rocket engines and gas generators, aviation power supplies and avionics also involved in high energy pulse power systems and their use in nuclear weapons effect testing. Common job positions include: Electrical Engineer; Mechanical Engineer; Physicist. Principal educational backgrounds sought: Engineering; Physics. Company benefits include: medical insurance; dental insurance; pension plan; life insurance; tuition assistance; disability coverage; savings plan. Corporate headquarters located in Stamford, CT. Parent company is Olin. Operationa at this facility

include: divisional headquarters; manufacturing; research/development; administration; service; sales.

THE OLYMPIAN
1268 East 4th Avenue, Olympia WA 98506. 206/754-5491. Contact Ann Engle, Personnel Director. Publishes an area newspaper with a circulation of over 25,000. A member of the Gannett Newspapers Group. Common positions include: Accountant; Administrator; Blue-Collar Worker Supervisor; Commercial Artist; Computer Programmer; Credit Manager; Customer Service Representative; Department Manager; Operations/Production Manager; Marketing Specialist; Personnel & Labor Relations Specialist; Public Relations Worker; Reporter/Editor; Sales Representative; Technical Writer/Editor. Principal educational backgrounds sought: Accounting; Art/Design; Business Administration; Communications; Computer Science; Finance; Marketing. Company benefits include: medical, dental, and life insurance; pension plan; tuition assistance; disability coverage; employee discounts; savings plan. Corporate headquarters location: Rosslyn, VA. New York Stock Exchange.

OLYMPIC CAPITAL MANAGEMENT
3008 Rainier Tower, Seattle WA 98101. 206/447-9399. Contact Personnel Department. A prominent Seattle investment advisory company.

OLYMPIC HOMECARE PRODUCTS COMPANY
2233 112th Avenue North East, Bellevue WA 98004. 206/453-1700. Contact Nan Cornehl, Personnel

Department. A major manufacturer of Olympic stain, overcoat, weather screen, primecoat, lucite paints.

OLYMPIC SALES, INC.
P.O. Box 7130, Seattle WA 98133. 206/522-2142. Contact Personnel Department. A main Seattle retailer of boats.

OPCON, INC.
720 80th Street Southwest, Everett WA 98203. 206/353-0900. Contact Human Resources Department. A manufacturer of a wide variety of electronics equipment, including data processing systems and products and a line of communications equipment.

OROWEAT BAKERS
1604 North 34th Street, Seattle WA 98103. 206/634-2700. Contact Personnel Department. A company which produces a variety of baked goods for commercial distribution. Parent company: General Foods Corporation. Corporate headquarters location: White Plains, NY.

PABST BREWING COMPANY
Custer Way & Schmidt Place, P.O. Box 947, Olympia WA 98507. 206/754-5000. Contact Alice Riley, Personnel Director. A company which produces a line of widely-distributed beers and malt beverages.

PACCAR, INC.
777 106th Avenue Northeast, Bellevue WA 98004. 206/455-7400. Contact Ingrid Rasch, Director of Human Resources & Planning. A major manufacturer

of heavy duty trucks and other equipment for industrial and commercial use. Brand names include Peterbilt and Kenworth. Corporate headquarters location.

PACIFIC COAST FEATHER COMPANY, INC.
1964 4th Avenue, Seattle WA 98134. 206/624-1057. Contact Personnel Department. A key Seattle company engaged in the manufacture of house furnishings and features.

PACIFIC ELECTRO DYNAMICS
11465 Willows Road Northeast, P.O. Box 97045, Redmond WA 98073-9745. 206/881-1700. Contact Melinda Wilson, Personnel Director. A company which manufactures a wide variety of electronics components and systems, including measurement devices for industrial applications.

PACIFIC FIRST FEDERAL
1519 4th Avenue, Seattle WA 98101. 206/382-7500. Contact Personnel Department. A leading Seattle bank holding company.

PACIFIC FIRST FEDERAL SAVINGS BANK
P.O. Box 1257, Tacoma WA 98401. 206/383-7658. Contact Kathy A. Philby, Assistant V.P./Employment Coordinator. A company which offers a wide range of financial services to area customers. Common positions include: Accountant; Bank Officer/Manager; Computer Programmer; Customer Service Representative. Principal educational backgrounds sought: Accounting; Business Administration; Computer Science; Finance; Marketing. Company benefits include: medical

insurance; pension plan; life insurance; disability coverage; profit sharing; savings plan. Corporate, regional, and divisional headquarters location. Operations at this facility include: administration. New York Stock Exchange.

PACIFIC INTERNATIONAL CORPORATION
511 7th Avenue South, Seattle WA 98104. 206/624-0137. Contact Personnel Department. A primary Seattle real estate leasor of restaurant cocktail lounges.

PACIFIC NORTHWEST BELL
1600 Bell Plaza, Room 3214, Seattle WA 98191. 206/345-4593. Contact Personnel Department. A leading service company engaged in telecommunications services.

PACIFIC TELECOM, INC.
805 Broadway, Vancouver WA 98660. 206/696-0983. Contact Bob Kemp, Personnel Director. A holding company providing administrative and other services to subsidiary companies, whose operations include providing telephone service to customers.

PACIFIC TRAIL SPORTSWEAR
1310 Mercer Street, Seattle WA 98109. 206/622-8730. Contact Personnel Department. A company engaged in the manufacturer of mens, boys, womens, and girls outerwear and sportwear.

PAINE CORPORATION
2401 South Bayview Street, Seattle WA 98144. 206/329-8600. Contact Personnel Department. A prominent

Seattle company engaged in the manufacture of pressure measuring instruments and thick film microcircuits.

PALMER GROUP
530 36th Avenue East, Seattle WA 98112. 206/628-8980. Contact Personnel Department. A main Seattle small business venture capital company.

PARSONS BRINCKERHOFF
710 Second Avenue, Suite 960, Seattle WA 98104. 206/624-3571. Contact Personnel Director. An engineering and design firm with operations in the design of bridges, tunnels, rapid transit systems, hydroelectric facilities, water supply systems, and marine facilities. Maintains regional and branch offices throughout the United States and abroad. Corporate headquarters location: New York, NY. New York Stock Exchange.

PAY 'N PAC STORES, INC.
1209 South Central, Kent WA 98032. 206/854-5450. Contact Barbara Collette, Personnel Director. A company which operates a chain of retail home supply stores, featuring such items as hardware, plumbing goods, electrical items, and building materials.

PAYN SAVE, INC.
4045 Delridge Way South West, P.O. Box C-47255, Seattle WA 98146. 206/938-6500. Contact Personnel Department. A primary Seattle company engaged in drug sundries and general merchandise.

PEANUT BUTTER PUBLISHING

329 Second Avenue West, Seattle WA 98119. 206/281-5965. Contact Gail Anrig, Office Manager. An area publisher specializing in cookbooks and dining-out guides. Common positions include: Accountant; Advertising Worker; Commercial Artist; Editor; Food Technologist; Graphic Designer; Marketing Specialist; Proofreader; Public Relations Worker. Principal educational backgrounds sought: Art/Design; Communications; Marketing. Company benefits include: medical, dental and life insurance; pension plan. Corporate headquarters location.

PENINSULA DAILY NEWS

P.O. Box 1330, Port Angeles WA 98362. 206/452-2345. Contact Managing Editor. A company which publishes an area newspaper with a circulation of over 10,000. A member of Persis Corp. Common positions include: Journalist. Principal educational backgrounds sought: Liberal Arts; Journalism. Corporate headquarters location: Honolulu, HI.

PENINSULA PLYWOOD

439 Marine Drive, Port Angeles WA 98362. 206/457-4421. Contact Doug McInnes, Personnel Director. A manufacturer of forest products for use in home applications, including exterior siding. Employs approximately 300 people.

PEOPLES NATIONAL BANK OF WASHINGTON

P.O. Box 720, Seattle WA 98111-0720. 206/344-2300. Contact Human Resources. An area financial institution offering a wide range of financial services to its customers.

PETER PAN SEAFOODS, INC.
1000 Denny Building, Sixth & Blanchard, Seattle WA 98121. 206/728-6000. Contact Cathy Wingert, Personnel Manager. Processes and distributes a variety of canned, fresh, and frozen seafood products, including salmon, halibut, cod, crab, etc. Common positions include: Accountant; Advertising Worker; Claim Representative; Computer Programmer; Credit Manager; Customer Service Representative; Food Technologist; Department Manager; General Manager; Operations/Production Manager; Personnel & Labor Relations Specialist; Public Relations Worker; Purchasing Agent; Quality Control Supervisor; Sales Representative; Transportation & Traffic Specialist. Company benefits include: medical insurance; dental insurance; pension plan; life insurance; tuition assistance; disability coverage; profit sharing; employee discounts; savings plan.

PETS, INC.
P.O. Box 95879, Seattle WA 98145. 206/525-1700. Contact Personnel Department. A prominent property owner, manager, and developer company.

PHYSIO-CONTROL CORPORATION
11811 Willows Road North East, P.O. Box 97006-9706, Redmond WA 98073. 206/867-4000. Contact Human Resources Department. A manufacturer of acute cardiac care components and related medical equipment, including monitors, peritoneal dialysis

systems, and defibrillators. A subsidiary of Eli Lilly & Company. Corporate headquarters location: Indianapolis, IN.

PIERRE ENTERPRISES, INC.
1152 Lake City Way North East, Seattle WA 98125. 206/364-2200. Contact Personnel Department. A prime Seattle company engaged in retail leases and rents

PIZZA HAVEN, INC.
12860 Inter Urban South Avenue, Seattle WA 98168. 206/241-2990. Contact Personnel Department. A leading chain of pizza restaurants

PLUM CREEK LUMBER COMPANY, INC.
999 Third Avenue, Suite 2300, Seattle WA 98104. 206/467-3600. Contact Personnel Department. A leading Seattle company engaged in the manufacture of softwood and hardwood, lumber, plywood, fiber bands, and laminates.

PNS, INC.
4045 Delridge Way SW, Seattle WA 98146. 206/938-6500. Contact Personnel Department. A major Seattle company engaged in the manufacture of drugs, drug sundries, and general merchandise.

PRECOR U.S.A., INC.
P.O. Box 3004, Bothell WA 98052. 206/486-9292. Contact Personnel Department. A manufacturer of exercise equipment.

PRESERVATIVE PAINT COMPANY
5410 Airport Ways, Seattle WA 98108. 206/763-0300. Contact Personnel Department. A leading Seattle company engaged in the manufacture and retail of consumer maintenance contractor and industrial paint coatings.

PRESTON RIDGE FINANCIAL SERVICES CORP.
1101 Second Avenue, Seattle WA 98101. 206/464-4810. Contact Personnel Department. A leading Seattle real estate development corporation.

PRICE WATERHOUSE
1001 4th Avenue Plaza, Suite 4200, Seattle WA 98154. 206/622-1505. Contact Fred Raney, Personnel Director. Nationally, the firm is one of the largest public accounting firms in the United States, with offices in 67 cities across the country and more than 290 offices in approximately 90 countries. Positions on the firm's professional staff provide opportunities to learn the administration and fiscal policies of companies representing a cross-section of American industry. Corporate headquarters location: New York, NY.

PRIME CONSTRUCTION COMPANY, INC.
8523 15th Avenue North East, Seattle WA 98125. 206/524-9200. Contact Personnel Department. A major Seattle warehouse and commercial building contractor.

PRINCESS TOURS
2815 2nd Avenue, Suite 400, Seattle WA 98121. 206/728-4202. Contact Personnel Department. A major provider of air, land, and ship tours.

PROCTOR & ASSOCIATES COMPANY
15050 Northeast 36th Street, Redmond WA 98052. 206/881-7000. Contact Human Resources Department. A manufacturer of telephone equipment classified as station apparatus, central office equipment, test equipment, and retail telephone accessories. Corporate headquarters location. Operations at this facility include: manufacturing; research/development; administration; service; sales. Common positions include: Accountant; Administrator; Buyer; Computer Programmer; Customer Service Representative; Draftsperson; Electronic Engineer; Software Engineer; Department Manager; General Manager; Operations/Production Manager; Marketing Specialist; Personnel & Labor Relations Specialist; Programmer; Purchasing Agent; Quality Control Supervisor; Sales Representative; Technical Writer/Editor. Principal educational background sought: Engineering. Company benefits include: medical insurance; dental insurance; profit sharing; life insurance; tuition assistance.

PRUDENTIAL INSURANCE COMPANY OF AMERICA
19009 33rd Avenue West, Suite 305, WA . 206/775-7258. Contact District Manager. Nationally, the firm is one of the world's largest multiline insurance companies, with home offices throughout the United States and Canada. Controls assets of $75 billion;

established 1875. Corporate headquarters location: Newark, NJ.

PUBLIC EMPLOYEES MUTUAL INSURANCE
325 East Lake, Seattle WA 98109. 206/628-4000. Contact Personnel Department. A leading Seattle company involved in casualty property and auto insurance underwriting.

PUGET SOUND BANCORP
1119 Pacific Avenue, Tacoma WA 98402. 206/593-3790. Contact Tex Whitney, Personnel Director. A bank holding company whose subsidiaries offer a wide range of financial services. Employs over 1,000 people.

PUGET SOUND FREIGHT LINES, INC.
P.O. Box 24526, Seattle WA 98124. 206/623-1600. Contact Assistant Controller. A company engaged, through subsidiary operations, in water surface transport and related freight moving activities.

PUGET SOUND POWER & LIGHT COMPANY
OBC-15, One Bellevue Center, P.O. Box 97034, Bellevue WA 98009. 206/454-6363. Contact Mrs. Bernadene Dochnahl, Director of Human Resources. An investor-owned electric utility serving more than 1.4 million people within a 4,500-square-mile service area that includes eight counties bordering Puget Sound in western Washington and one county in central Washington. Corporate headquarters location.

QUINTON INSTRUMENTS COMPANY
2121 Terry Avenue, Seattle WA 98121. 206/223-7373. Contact Industrial Relations Department. A company which manufactures electronic medical instruments for a number of applications.

RAINIER BANCORP
Rainier Bank Tower, P.O. Box 3966, Seattle WA 98124. 206/621-4111. Contact Donald B. Summers, Senior Vice President. Manager of Personnel Administration. A company which provides a wide range of financial services to area customers. Employs over 5,000 people. Common positions include: Accountant; Advertising; Attorney; Bank Officer/Manager; Computer Programmer; Credit Manager; Customer Service Representative; Economist; Financial Analyst; Marketing Specialist; Personnel & Labor Relations Specialist; Programmer; Purchasing Agent; Systems Analyst; Technical Writer/Editor. Principal educational backgrounds sought: Accounting; Business Administration; Computer Science; Economics; Finance; Marketing. Company benefits include: medical insurance; dental insurance; pension plan; life insurance; tuition assistance; disability coverage; profit sharing; employee discounts; savings plan.

RAINIER BREWING COMPANY
3100 Airport Way South, Seattle WA 98134. 206/622-2600. Contact John Mack, Personnel Director. A company which produces a widely-distributed line of beers and ales. A wholly-owned subsidiary of the G. Heileman Brewing Company; employs over 400 people.

RAINIER NATIONAL BANK
1301 Fifth Avenue, Seattle WA 98101. 206/621-4024. Contact Personnel Department. A leading financial services company.

RALEIGH CYCLE COMPANY OF AMERICA
22710 72nd Street South, Kent WA 98032. 206/395-1100. Contact Personnel Department. A major distributer of Raleigh bicycles, accessories, and cycling clothing.

RATELCO, INC.
1260 Mercer Street, Seattle WA 98109. 206/624-7770. Contact Lisa McLean, Personnel. A manufacturer of a wide variety of electronics equipment, components, and systems.

RECREATIONAL EQUIPMENT, INC.
6750 South 228th, Kent WA 98032. 206/395-3780. Contact Diane Kovacs, Employment Supervisor. A major specialty retailer of outdoor apparel and recreational equipment. Presently REI has 17 stores and a large mail order business. Products include: bikes, skis, kayaks, backpacking and climbing gear, sportswear, and inclement weather clothing. Corporate headquarters location. Common positions include: Accountant; Administrator; Advertising Worker; Blue-Collar Worker Supervisor; Buyer; Commercial Artist; Computer Programmer; Credit Manager; Customer Service Representative; Financial Analyst; Manager; Department Manager; Operations/Production Manager; Marketing Specialist; Personnel & Labor

Relations Specialist; Programmer; Public Relations Worker; Purchasing Agent; Systems Analyst; Technical Writer/Editor. Principal educational backgrounds sought: Accounting; Art/Design; Communications; Computer Science. Company benefits include: medical insurance; dental insurance; pension plan; life insurance; tuition assistance; disability coverage; profit sharing; employee discounts. Corporate, regional and divisional headquarters location. Operations include: research/development; administration; sales.

RED CEDAR SHINGLE & HAND-SPLIT
Shake Bureau, 575 116th Avenue, North East, NO. 275, Bellevue WA 98004. 206/453-1323. Contact Linda Harrington, Personnel Department. A major producer of certigrade red cedar shingles, certigroove grooved shakes,and certi-split handsplit shakes.

RESTAURANTS UNLIMITED, INC.
1818 North Northlake Way, Seattle WA 98103. 206/634-0550. Contact Tom Griffith, Personnel Department. Owners and operators of a leading chain of restaurants. Common job positions include: Restaurant Manager; Executive Chef/Kitchen Manager. Principal educational backgrounds sought: Business Administration; Communications; Economics; Liberal Arts; Hotel and Restaurant Management. Company benefits include: medical insurance; dental insurance; life insurance; disability coverage; profit sharing; employee discounts; clothing; auto. Corporate headquarters. Operations at this facility include: regional headquarters; divisional headquarters; administration.

ROCKCOR, INC.
11441 Willows Road, P.O. Box 97073-9709, Redmond WA 98052. 206/885-5000. Contact Director/Human Resources & Communication. A company which develops and produces advanced technology products in the fields of rocket research, aerospace and defense, energy, telecommunications, and other high-technology areas. Employs approximately 1200 people. Corporate and divisional headquarters location. Common positions include: Accountant; Administrator; Attorney; Blue Collar Worker Supervisor; Buyer; Chemist; Computer Programmer; Draftsperson; Engineer; Aerospace Engineer; Chemical Engineer; Mechanical Engineer; Financial Analyst; Personnel & Labor Relations Specialist; Programmer; Quality Control Supervisor; Technical Writer/Editor. Principal educational backgrounds sought: appropriate degree.

ROCKET RESEARCH COMPANY
OLIN DEFENSE GROUP
11441 Willows Road, P.O. Box 97009, Redmond WA 98073-9709. 206/885-5000. Contact Mr. John Knapp, Employment Manager. A major manufacturer of comp-mono propellant, hydrazine rocket engines, and gas generators.

ROFFE, INC. D/B/A ROFFEE
808 Howell Street, Seattle WA 98101. 206/622-0456. Contact Personnel Department. A major manufacturer of ski-wear.

ROHR BACK CORPORATION
2200 6th Avenue, Suite 833, Seattle WA 98121. 206/441-6616. Contact Personnel Department. A leading Seattle company engaged in the manufacture of corrosion measurement and control instruments.

ROMAN MEAL COMPANY
2101 South Tacoma Way, Tacoma WA 98409. 206/475-0964. Contact Personnel Department. A company which produces and markets whole grain bakery, natural products, and bakery goods.

ROSAVER'S SUPERMARKETS
North 7511 Freya, Spokane WA 99220. 509/467-2620. Contact Personnel Department. A leading chain of supermarkets

SAFECARE COMPANY, INC.
900 4th Avenue, Seattle WA 98164. 206/223-4560. Contact Personnel Department. A leading Seattle research and development, and investment company.

SAFECO CORPORATION
Safeco Plaza, Seattle WA 98185. 206/545-5000. Contact Dennis McCormick, Personnel. Offers a wide range of insurance services, including property and casualty, life and health, and title insurance lines. Also engaged in such related areas of activity as data processing/accounting systems sales, a credit company, and a real estate development company. Corporate headquarters location.

THE SEATTLE JOB BANK

SANDILANDS WURZ HAFELI LOGES
720 Olive Way, Seattle WA 98101. 206/343-7905. Contact Personnel Department. A major Seattle advertising agency.

SAVINGS BANK OF PUGET SOUND
815 2nd Avenue, Seattle WA 98104. 206/447-5700. Contact Personnel Department. A leading Seattle bank.

SCA WOLFF SYSTEM
12421 Willows Road North East, P.O. Box 97015/98083, Kirkland WA 98034. 206/821-1133. Contact Personnel Department. Company specializing in the service and distribution of tanning and toning equipment.

SCHUCK'S AUTO SUPPLY
15395 South East 30th Plaza Suite 220, Bellevue WA 98007. 206/644-2002. Contact Personnel Department. Office of retail auto parts and access stores.

SCOTT PAPER COMPANY/ NORTHWEST OPERATIONS
P.O. Box 925, Everett WA 98206. 206/259-7333. Contact Mark Fanning, Human Resources Manager. A major area processor of pulp and paper, operating facilities for manufacturing such products as facial tissues, napkins, and paper towels. Extensive timberland operations. Corporate headquarters location: Philadelphia, PA.

SEAFIRST CORPORATION

800 Fifth Avenue, 33rd Floor, Seattle WA 98124. Mailed inquiries only. Contact College Relations Coordinator. A financial services firm engaged in such activities as: trust; mortgage; corporate cash management; securities; and wholesale and retail lending. A subsidiary of BankAmerica Corporation. Employs 7,000 in the United States. Common positions include: Accountant; Bank Officer/Manager; Computer Programmer; Credit Manager; Financial Analyst; Branch Manager; Department Manager; Management Trainee; Operations/Production Manager; Marketing Specialist; Personnel & Labor Relations Specialist; Programmer; Systems Analyst. Principal educational backgrounds sought: Accounting; Business Administration; Computer Science; Economics; Finance; Liberal Arts; Marketing. Company benefits include: medical insurance; dental insurance; pension plan; life insurance; tuition assistance; disability coverage; employee discounts; savings plan; group legal.

SEA FIRST MORTGAGE CORPORATION

701 5th Avenue, Seattle WA 98104. 206/358-7800. Contact Personnel Department. A leading area mortgage banker company.

SEA GALLEY RESTAURANTS

6920 220th South West, Mountlake, Terrace WA 98043. 206/775-0411. Contact Suzanne Scharz, Vice President. Operates 40 full service dinner house restaurants in Washington, Oregon, Arkansas, Colorado, and Wyoming. Common job positions include: Food Technologist; Manager/Assistant Manager; Restaurant

Manager; Kitchen Manager. Principal educational backgrounds sought: Business Administration; Marketing. Company benefits include: medical insurance; dental insurance; life insurance; tuition assistance; disability coverage; employee discounts; savings plan. Corporate headquarters. Operations at this facility include: regional headquarters; administration.

SEA-LAND SERVICE, INC.
3600 Port of Tacoma Road, Tacoma WA 98424. 206/593-8042. Contact J.A. Van Housen, Personnel Manager. One of the nation's largest container shipping companies, with operations extending to major harbors and industrial centers around the world. Common positions include: Blue-Collar Worker Supervisor; Sales Representative; Transportation & Traffic Specialist. Principal educational backgrounds sought: Business Administration; Marketing. Company benefits include: medical, dental, and life insurance; pension plan; tuition assistance; disability coverage; employee discounts; savings plan. Divisional headquarters location. Operations at this facility include: administration; service; sales. Corporate headquarters location: Menlo Park, NJ. New York Stock Exchange.

SEATTLE CITY LIGHT
DEPT. OF CITY OF SEATTLE
1015 Third Avenue, Seattle WA 98104. 206/625-3000. Contact Personnel Department. A major municipal electric utility.

SEATTLE DAILY JOURNAL OF COMMERCE
P.O. Box 11050, Seattle WA 98111. 206/622-8272. Contact John Mihalyo, General Manager. A company which publishes an area daily newspaper with a circulation of approximately 5,000.

SEATTLE-FIRST NATIONAL BANK
P.O. Box 3977, Seattle WA 98124. 206/583-3131. Contact Gloria Phurlow, Employment. A full service commercial bank. Services include trusts, investments, international banking, and data processing. 170 locations throughout Washington. Corporate headquarters location.

SEATTLE MARINE FISHING SUPPLY COMPANY
2121 West Commodore Way, Seattle WA 98199. 206/285-5010. Contact Personnel Department. A leading company engaged in the wholesale of marine supplies and hardware.

SEATTLE NORTHWEST SECURITY CORPORATION
800 5th Avenue, Seattle WA 98104. 206/628-2882. Contact Personnel Department. A leading area security brokerage and dealership company.

SEATTLE PACIFIC INDUSTRIES, INC.
P.O. Box 58710, Seattle WA 98138. 206/282-8889. Contact Personnel Department. A leading company engaged in the manufacture, design, and wholesale of clothing.

SEATTLE POST-INTELLIGENCER
521 Wall Street, Seattle WA 98121. Mailed inquries only. Contact Tom Sellers, City Editor. Publishes a daily newspaper as part of the Hearst Newspapers Group; weekday circulation exceeds 190,000; more than 469,000 on Sunday. Competitor The Seattle Times conducts circulation, advertising, and production operations for this paper.

SEATTLE STEEL
P.O. Box C-3827, Seattle WA 98124. 206/938-6800. Contact George Yelland, Personnel Director. A major area processor of steel and related metals products, including bolts, fasteners, and track spikes.

THE SEATTLE TIMES
P.O. Box 70, Seattle WA 98111. Mailed inquiries only. Contact Personnel Manager. Publishes an independent daily newspaper. Weekday circulation exceeds 225,000; more than 469,000 on Sunday. Circulation, advertising, and production operations for competitor Seattle Post-Intelligencer are also conducted here. Corporate headquarters location. Common positions include: Advertising Worker; Computer Programmer; Department Manager; Operations/Production Manager; Reporter/Editor; Sales Representative. Principal educational backgrounds sought: Business Administration; Communications; Liberal Arts; Marketing. Company benefits include: medical insurance; dental insurance; pension plan; savings plan.

THE SEATTLE JOB BANK

SEATTLE TIMES COMPANY
1120 John Street, Seattle WA 98109. 206/464-2111. Contact Personnel Department. A leading newspaper company.

SEATTLE TRUST & SAVINGS BANK
P.O. Box 90, Seattle WA 98111. 206/223-2043. Contact Rosalie Powell, Employment Manager. A medium sized commercial bank providing quality products/service to consumer and commercial customers in the Puget Sound area, through Personal Banking, Corporate Banking, Mortgage Banking, and Trust divisions. Branches throughout the Puget Sound area. Corporate headquarters location. Common positions include: Accountant; Bank Officer/Manager; Buyer; Credit Manager; Customer Service Representative; Finance; Marketing. Company benefits include: medical insurance; dental insurance; pension plan; life insurance; tuition assistance; disabilty coverage; profit sharing; employee discounts; savings plan; vacation; holidays.

SELLEN CONSTRUCTION COMPANY, INC.
228 9th Avenue North, P.O. Box 9970, Seattle WA 98109. 206/682-7770. Contact Personnel Department. A prominent general contractor of nonresidential and industrial buildings.

SHAKERTOWN CORPORATION
1220 Kerran Street, Winlock WA 98596. 206/785-3501. Contact Personnel Department. A leading manufacturer of cedar shingle siding panels, cedar shingle roofing panels.

SHANNON & WILSON
1105 North 38th Street, P.O. Box C-30313, Seattle WA 98103. 206/632-8020. Contact Earl Sibley, President. A company which provides geotechnical consulting services to a variety of industrial and governmental clients. Services include foundation engineering studies, waste management, and construction monitoring. Corporate headquarters location.

SHARP HARTWIG ADVERTISING
South Tower 100 West Harrison Plaza, Suite 500, Seattle WA 98119. 206/282-6242. Contact Office Manager. An area advertising agency offering a variety of services.

SHELL OIL COMPANY
P.O. Box 700, Anacortes WA 98221. 206/293-9119. Contact Personnel Director. AN area refinery engaged in the production of automobile and airplane fuels, including kerosene and diesel products. Nationally, the firm is involved in the exploration for, and the development, production, purchase, transportation, and marketing of, crude oil, natural gas, petroleum products, and related chemical products. Corporate headquarters location: Houston, TX. New York Stock Exchange.

SHEPARD AMBULANCE, INC.
1140 12th Avenue, Seattle WA 98122. 206/322-0330. Contact Human Resources. A premier Seattle service company providing ambulance services. Common positions include: Accountant; Credit Manager; Customer Service Representative; Personnel & Labor

Relations Specialist; Public Relations Worker; Purchasing Agent; Systems Analyst; Emergency Medical Technician; Dispatcher. Principal educational backgrounds sought: Accounting; Computer Science; Emergency Medical Technician. Company benefits include: medical insurance; dental insurance; pension plan; life insurance. Corporate headquarters are located in Newport Beach, CA. Parent company SecoAmerica, Inc. Operations at this facility include: Service.

SIGMA RESEARCH, INC.
8710 148th Avenue Northeast, Redmond WA 98052. 206/883-9217. Contact Personnel Manager. A company which manufactures precision optical equipment and related components for a variety of scientific and research and development applications.

THE SIMPSON DOOR COMPANY
P.O. Box 210, 400 Simpson Avenue, McClearly WA 98557. 206/495-3291. Contact Personnel Department. A major manufacturer of doors.

SIMPSON INVESTMENT COMPANY
1201 3rd Avenue, Seattle WA 98101-3009. 206/224-5000. Contact Human Resources. A major producer of lumber products, paper, and PVC extruded plastic pipe. Common positions include: Accountant; Computer Programmer; Forester; Personnel & Labor Relations Specialist; Quality Control Supervisor; Sales Representative; Systems Analyst. Principal educational backgrounds sought: Accounting; Business Administration; Engineering; Finance. Company

benefits include: medical insurance; dental insurance; pension plan; life insurance; tuition assistance; disability coverage; savings plan. Corporate headquarters location. Operations at this facility include: administration; sales.

SIMPSON TIMBER COMPANY
1201 3rd Avenue Suite 4900, Seattle WA 98101-3009. 206/292-5000. Contact Personnel Department. A major Seattle company engaged in the manufacture of hardwood.

SKAGIT VALLEY HERALD
1000 East College Way, P.O. Box 578, Mount Vernon WA 98273. 206/424-3251. Contact Carl Molesworth, Editor. A company which publishes an area newspaper with a circulation of over 16,000. A member of the Pioneer Newspapers group. Common positions include: Advertising Worker; Commercial Artist; Reporter/Editor. Principal educational backgrounds sought: Art/Design; Communications; Liberal Arts; Marketing. Company benefits include: medical insurance; pension plan.

SKIPPER'S, INC.
14450 North East 29th Place, Bellevue WA 98007. 206/885-2116. Contact Anna Iorganides, Human Resources. A fast food seafood restaurant chain.

SKOWL ARM TIMBER CORPORATION
One Union Square, Seattle WA 98101. 206/624-6166. Contact Personnel Department. A primary Seattle sawmill.

SKYWAY LUGGAGE COMPANY
#10 Wall Street, Seattle WA 98121-1392. 206/441-5300. Contact Personnel Department. A key manufacturer of luggage, trucks, and bags.

SNOKIST GROWERS
P.O. Box 1587, Yakima WA 98907. 509/453-5631. Contact Personnel. An area fruit processor, with operations in plums, apples, cherries, and other items. Employs approximately 400 people.

SOUTHLAND CORPORATION
1035 Andover Park West, Tukwila WA 98188. 206/575-6711. Contact Diana Cotterell, Personnel Director. A major processor of dairy products, distributed under 11 regional brand names. Also operates more than 6,800 7-Eleven stores worldwide, as well as numerous other food and sandwich stores, auto parts stores, self-service gasoline outlets, and numerous processing and distribution centers. Corporate headquarters location: Dallas, TX. New York Stock Exchange.

SOUTHWOOD MANOR
12571 A Corliss Avenue Northh, Seattle WA 98133. 206/364-1617. Contact Personnel Department. A prominent mobile home park in Seattle.

SPACELABS, INC.
4200 150th Avenue, North East, P.O. Box 97013, Redmond WA 98073. 206/882-3700. Contact Personnel Department. A manufacturer of patient monitoring

equipment, clinical information systems, ambulatory monitoring products, and monitoring supplies.

SPECIALTY FOODS INTERNATIONAL
701 Dexter Avenue North, 410A, Seattle WA 98109. 206/656-2855. Contact Personnel Department. An international food company specializing in gourmet and specialty natural foods; distributor to 9 states in the Northwest.

SPOKANE DIVISION/ HEWLETT PACKARD
East 24001 Mission Avenue, Spokane WA 99220. Mailed inquiries only. Contact Personnel Department. Produces RF (radio frequency) signal generators and synthesizers, RF measuring receivers and RF transceiver test equipment. Parent company, Hewlett Packard, is engaged in the design and manufacture of measurement and computation products and systems used in business, industry, engineering, science, health care, and education; principal products are integrated instrument and computer systems (including hardware and software), computer systems and peripheral products, and medical electronic equipment and systems.

THE SPOKESMAN-REVIEW & SPOKANE CHRONICLE
West 999 Riverside, Spokane WA 99210. 509/459-5000. Contact Personnel Department. The office of a leading area newspaper.

THE SEATTLE JOB BANK

SPORTCASTER COMPANY
P.O. Box 4370, Seattle WA 98104. 206/587-0327. Contact Personnel Department. Importer of mens, ladies, and childrens unlined insulated sportswear.

SPRAGUE RESOURCES CORPORATION
425 Pontius Avenue North, Seattle WA 98109. 206/447-7545. Contact Personnel Department. A principal Seattle holding company.

SQUARE D COMPANY
South 1604 Garfield Road, Airway Heights WA 99001. 509/244-5661. Contact Bob Schrader, Personnel Director. A major manufacturer of wiring components, switchgear, and related items. Corporate headquarters location: Palatine, IL.

STADELMAN FRUIT, INC.
314 South Second Avenue, Yakima WA 98902. 509/452-8571. Contact Larry Lembeck, Personnel Director. An area fruit packer and wholesaler. Products include apples, pears, cherries, apricots, prunes, and plums.

STEPAN & ASSOCIATES
33505 13th Place South, Federal Way WA 98003. 206/927-7850. Contact Gary Gray, Office Manager. A company which offers specialized environmental engineering services to a variety of clients in government and industry. A subsidiary of Engineering-Science Companies. Corporate headquarters location: Arcadia, CA.

THE SEATTLE JOB BANK

STEVENSON CO-PLY, INC.
P.O. Box 910, Stevenson WA 98648. 509/427-5621. Contact Office Manager. An area producer of plywood and related lumber products.

THE STIMPSON CLARK, INC.
83 South King Street, Seattle WA 98107. 201/583-8118. Contact Personnel Department. A prominent Seattle advertising agency.

STRATEGIC DIRECT
83 South King Street Suite 815, Seattle WA 98104. 206/467-1500. Contact Personnel Department. A leading advertising agency.

SUNDSTRAND DATA CONTROL, INC.
15001 Northeast 36th Street, P.O. Box 97001, Redmond WA 98073. 206/885-3711. Contact Joe Luce, Manager/Employee Relations. A company engaged in the production of aircraft equipment and parts including temperature control components, digital recorders, and a variety of instrumentation systems. Employs over 1000 people. Group headquarters location. Operations at this facility include: manufacturing; administration; service; sales. Common positions include: Accountant; Administrator; Computer Programmer; Customer Service Representative; Engineer; Aerospace Engineer; Electrical Engineer; Industrial Engineer; Mechanical Engineer; Financial Analyst; Manager; Department Manager; General Manager; Operations/Production Manager; Personnel & Labor Relations Specialist; Programmer; Purchasing Agent; Quality Control

Supervisor; Systems Analyst; Technical Writer/Editor. Principal educational backgrounds sought: Accounting; Business Administration; Computer Science; Engineering; Finance; Mathematics. Company benefits include: medical insurance; dental insurance; pension plan; life insurance; tuition assistance; savings plan.

SUNNYSIDE DAILY NEWS
520 South Seventh, P.O. Box 878, Sunnyside WA 98944. 509/837-4500. Contact Tom Lanctot, Personnel Director. The publisher of an area daily newspaper.

SUNRISE RESORT & RECREATION
437 41st Street South West, P.O. Box 4100, Renton WA 98057. 206/656-2861. Contact Personnel Department. A prime operator of a vehicle campground in the Seattle area.

TACOMA BOATBUILDING COMPANY
1840 Marine View Drive, Tacoma WA 98422. 206/572-3600. Contact Charles Holmes, Employment Manager. A company engaged in shipbuilding activities for area clients; employs over 1,500 people.

TACOMA GOODWILL INDUSTRIES REHABILITATION CENTER, INC.
714 South 27th Street, Tacoma WA 98409. 206/272-5166. Contact Mr. John Ryan, Personnel. A company which provides human service and rehabilitation programs for employees through such activities as mail preparation and sorting, hand assembly projects, and metal and woodwork jobs for area clients. Employs over 500 people.

TACOMA NEWS TRIBUNE
1950 South State Street, Tacoma WA 98405. 206/597-8757. Contact Personnel Department. The office of a leading area newspaper.

P.J. TAGGARES COMPANY
1016 South Broadway, Othello WA 99344. 509/488-3356. Contact Dave Wiggins, Personnel. An area producer of a variety of potato products, including french fries. Corporate headquarters location.

TAMS CONSULTANTS
4401 First Interstate Center, 999 Third Avenue, Seattle WA 98104. 206/624-3532. Contact Dan Powell, Principal Associate. A company which provides professional consulting/engineering services to a variety of clients.

TAPCO
3810 148th Avenue Northeast, Redmond WA 98052. 206/881-9555. Contact Tom Classen, Personnel Director. A manufacturer of consumer electronics equipment and related items.

TELLER TRAINING INSTITUTES, INC.
400 VAL Building, 2033 Sixth Avenue, Seattle WA 98121. 206/448-7100. Contact Personnel Department. A major Seattle proprietary school.

TELTONE CORPORATION
10801 120th Avenue NE, Kirkland WA 98033. 206/827-9626. Contact Ms. Marnie Vitt, Personnel Manager. An

electronics manufacturer of telecommunications and data communications equipment. Employs approximately 300 people. Established in 1968. Common positions include: Accountant; Credit Manager; Customer Service Representative; Electrical Engineer; Industrial Engineer; Mechanical Engineer; Department Manager; Operations/Production Manager; Marketing Specialist; Personnel & Labor Specialist; Purchasing Agent; Quality Control Supervisor; Sales Representative; Systems Analyst; Technical Writer/Editor. Principal educational backgrounds sought: Accounting; Business Administration; Communications; Computer Science; Economics; Engineering; Finance; Marketing; Mathematics; Physics. Company benefits include: medical insurance; dental insurance; life insurance; tuition assistance; disability coverage; profit sharing; employee discounts; savings plan. Corporate headquarters location. Operations at this facility include: manufacturing; research & development; administration; service; sales.

TEMPRESS, INC.
701 South Orchard, Seattle WA 98108. 206/762-1419. Contact Personnel Department. A leading manufacturer of tools and die molds.

TENNYS TOYOTA, INC.
13355 Lake City Way, Seattle WA 98125. 206/367-0080. Contact Personnel Department. A main retailer and wholesaler of automobile parts and services.

THAI AIRWAYS INTERNATIONAL, LTD.
720 Olive Way, Suite 1400, Seattle WA 98101. 206/467-9898. Contact Personnel Department. A leading international passenger and freight air carrier company. Common job categories include: Accountant; Customer Service Representative; Sales Representative; Ticket Agent; Reservation and Sales Representative; Note: Flight Crews are only hired through Bangkok. Corporate headquarters are located in Bangkok, Thailand. Operations at this facility include regional headquarters.

THAW CORPORATION
P.O. Box 3978, Seattle WA 98124. 206/624-4277. Contact Personnel Department. A prominent Seattle manufacturer and importer of recreational products.

THOMPSON RECRUITMENT ADVERTISING, INC.
1511 Third Avenue, Suite 1000, Seattle WA 98101. 206/623-2620. Contact Denny Graham, Branch Manager. Nationally, the firm is an advertising agency specializing in personnel recruitment advertising, human resources management systems, and employee communications. Corporate headquarters location: Los Angeles, CA.

THRIFTY FOODS, INC.
P.O. Box 265, Burlington WA 98233. 206/757-1211. Contact Mr. Skiles, Personnel Director. A company which operates a chain of retail food stores with numerous local outlets.

TIME OIL COMPANY
2737 West Commodore Way, Seattle WA 98199. 206/2285-2400. Contact Personnel Department. A key Seattle company engaged in retail gasoline service stations, wholesale petroleum products, and retail fuel oil beaters.

TODD PACIFIC SHIPYARDS CORPORATION/ SEATTLE DIVISION
P.O. Box 3806, Seattle WA 98124. 206/623-1635. Contact Michael Marsh, Personnel Director. A company engaged in the construction and maintenance/repair of commercial ships, both domestic and foreign, and of ships for the U.S. Navy and other governmental agencies. Shipyards are strategically located in some of the nation's busiest ports where they meet the needs of international trade, intercoastal traffic, the offshore oil industry and inland waterway commerce. In addition to this location, the company operates facilities in a number of cities in the western and southern United States.

TODD SHIPYARDS CORPORATION
1801 16th Avenue South West, Seattle WA 98134. 206/623-1635. Contact Personnel Department. A leading Seattle company engaged in ship repair, conversion, and building.

TOLLYCRAFT YACHTS CORPORATION
2200 Clinton Avenue, Kelso WA 98626. 206/423-5160. Contact Personnel Department. A corporation specializing in the manufacturing of inboard motor yachts and cruisers.

TONE COMMANDER SYSTEMS, INC.
4320 150th Northeast, P.O. Box 97039, Redmond WA 98073-9739. 206/883-3600. Contact Marita Heckenkamp, Human Resources Manager. A manufacturer of telecommunications equipment, small PBX systems, and related electronic equipment. Common positions include: Accountant; Blue-Collar Worker Supervisor; Buyer; Draftsperson; Electrical Engineer; Marketing Specialist; Purchasing Agent; Quality Control Supervisor; Sales Representative; Technical Writer/Editor. Principal educational backgrounds sought: Business Administration; Engineering; Finance; Marketing. Company benefits include: medical, dental, and life insurance; pension plan; tuition reimbursement; disability coverage; savings plan. Corporate headquarters location. Operations at this facility include: manufacturing; research/development; administration; service; sales.

TRADEWELL STORES, INC.
Box 9500, Renton WA 98057. 206/235-8700. Contact Personnel. A company which operates an area retail grocery chain with over 100 outlets. Parent company: Pacific Gamble Robinson Company.

TRANSAMERICA TITLE INSURANCE
Park Place Building, 1200 Sixth Avenue, Seattle WA 98101. 206/628-4650. Contact Louise Condon, Personnel Director. Nationally, the firm is one of the nation's leading providers of title insurance, escrow, and other services relating to the transfer of real property. Direct operations are currently concentrated in nearly

100 counties in the western and southwestern states and Michigan. Also offers a complete tax service for mortgage lenders through subsidiary operations. Corporate headquarters location: San Francisco, CA.

TRAVELERS INSURANCE COMPANY
1200 6th Avenue, Seattle WA 98101. 206/464-3400. Contact Personnel Manager. Nationally, the firm is one of the largest investor-owned insurance and financial service institutions in the world. Writes every principal form of life, accident, health, and casualty/property insurance. Offers a broad range of pension and other investment management services. Operates more than 375 field offices throughout the country, and has assets of over $20 billion and more than $100 billion of life insurance in force. Corporate headquarters location: Hartford, CT. New York Stock Exchange.

TREE TOP, INC.
P.O. Box 248, Selah WA 98942. 509/697-7251. Contact Ron Flagg, Personnel Director. A major national processor of a wide variety of apple products, including juices and canned food products. Employs over 700 people. Corporate headquarters location.

TRI-CITY HERALD
P.O. Box 2608, Tri-Cities WA 99302. 509/582-1500. Contact Personnel Director. A company which publishes an area newspaper with a circulation of over 30,000. A member of the McClatchy Newspapers group.

TRIBUNE PUBLISHING COMPANY
P.O. Box 11000, 1950 South State Street, Tacoma WA 98411. 206/597-8575. Contact John J. Wilson, Director of Human Resources. The Publisher of the evening Tacoma News Tribune (circulation: 104,000), and the Sunday News-Tribune & Ledger (circulation exceeds 113,000). Corporate headquarters location. Common positions include: Advertising Worker; Computer Programmer; Credit Manager; Customer Service Representative; Manager; Marketing Specialist; Personnel & Labor Relations Specialist; Purchasing Agent; Reporter/Editor. Principal educational backgrounds sought: Business Administration; Liberal Arts; Marketing.

TWIN CITY FOODS, INC.
P.O. Box 699, 10120 269th Place Northwest, Stanwood WA 98292. 206/629-2111. Contact Don Heitman, Personnel Director. A major area processor of frozen vegetable products, including potatoes, carrots, and peas. Employs over 1,000 people.

TYCER FULTZ BELLACK/DAVIS
405 Columbia Street, Seattle WA 98104-1606. 206/386-5655. Contact Personnel Department. A major Seattle advertising agency.

U.S. BANK OF WASHINGTON
1414 4th Avenue, Seattle WA 98111. 206/344-5306. Contact Personnel Department. The third largest bank in Washington state. Common job positions include: Bank Officer/Manager; Customer Service Representative; Branch Manager; Department Manager. Principal educational backgrounds sought: Accounting; Business Administration; Communications; Economics; Finance; Liberal Arts. Company benefits include: medical insurance; dental insurance; pension plan; life insurance; tuition assistance; disabililty coverage; profit sharing; employee discounts; savings plan. Corporate headquarters. Parent company is U.S. Bancorporation. Operations at this facility include: regional headquarters; administration; service.

KEITH UDDENBERG, INC.
7520 Soundview Drive, P.O. Box 444, Gig Harbor WA 98335. 206/858-9108. Contact Connie Jackman, Personnel Director. A company operating a chain of retail grocery stores.

UI GROUP, INC.
P.O. Box 2308, Tri-Cities WA 99302. 509/735-6461. Contact Diane Kummer, Personnel Manager. A company engaged in the production and processing of a variety of food and farm goods, including frozen potatoes.

UNIFLITE, INC.
9th & Harris, P.O. Box 1095/98227, Bellingham WA 98225. 206/676-6200. Contact Darrell Markwood,

Personnel Department. A commercial and pleasure boat builder.

UNIGARD, INC.
1215 4th Avenue, Seattle WA 98161. 206/641-4321. Contact Personnel Department. A leading Seattle multiple line property and casualty insurance holding company.

UNIGARD INDEMMITY COMPANY, INC.
1215 4th Avenue, Seattle WA 98161. 206/641-4321. Contact Personnel Department. A principal Seattle insurance company specializing in fire, marine, and casualty insurance.

UNIGARD INSURANCE COMPANY
1215 4th Avenue, Seattle WA 98161. 206/641-4321. Contact Personnel Department. A key Seattle insurance company specializing in multiple line property and casualty insurance.

UNIGARD SERVICE CORPORATION
1215 Fourth Avenue, 18th Floor, Seattle WA 98161. 206/641-4321. Contact Personnel Department. A key Seattle company engaged in premium financing.

UNIMAR
1441 North Northlake Way, Seattle WA 98103. 206/632-1441. Contact Personnel Department. A main Seattle company engaged in ship building and repairing wholesale transportation equipment and supplies.

THE SEATTLE JOB BANK

UNISEA
P.O. Box 97019, 15110 Northeast 90th Street, Redmond WA 98073-9719. 206/881-8181. Contact Personnel. A major processor of seafood and related fishery items, including snow crab and salmon. Employs approximately 700 people.

UNITED GRAPHICS, INC.
1401 Broadway, Seattle WA 98122. 206/325-4400. Contact Personnel Department. A prominent Seattle company engaged in lithographic commercial printing.

UNITED PACIFIC INSURANCE
33405 8th Avenue South, Federal Way WA 98003. 206/952-5000. Contact Marilyn Hopper, Personnel Director. A company offering a line of insurance services to area customers. Corporate headquarters location.

UNITED PACIFIC LIFE INSURANCE COMPANY
33405 8th Avenue South, Federal Way WA 98003. 206/952-6770. Contact Personnel Department. A major life insurance company.

UNITED SAVINGS AND LOAN BANK
601 South Jackson, Seattle WA 98104. 206/624-7581. Contact Personnel Department. A principal Seattle savings and loan association.

UNIVAR CORPORATION
1600 Norton Building, 801 2nd Avenue, Seattle WA 98104. 206/447-5911. Contact Personnel Department. A multi-divisional company, engaged in four major lines

of industrial merchandising. Operates through the following units: Van Waters & Rogers, which distributes industrial chemicals throughout the United States; Van Waters & Rogers, Ltd., which distributes similar products throughout Canada, as well as certain agricultural chemicals in the Western Provinces; VWR Scientific, a major national distributor of a broad line of laboratory and graphic arts products; and VW&R Home Furnishings, which distributes supplies and fabrics to furniture and bedding manufacturers, reupholsterers, and the decorator/contract market. Corporate headquarters location. New York Stock Exchange. Common positions include: Accountant; Attorney; Draftsperson; Engineer; Department Manager. Principal educational backgrounds sought: Accounting; Business Administration; Engineering. Company benefits include: medical insurance; dental insurance; pension plan; life insurance; tuition assistance; disability coverage; employee discounts; savings plan.

UNIVERSAL SERVICES, INC.
520 Pike Street, P.O. Box 2230, Seattle WA 98106-4006. 206/340-9200. Contact Human Resources Manager. A catering firm offering prepared food and related services to area clients.

UNIVERSAL SERVICES, INC. - INTERNATIONAL
520 Pike Suite 2200, Seattle WA 98101. 206/340-9200. Contact Personnel Department. A primary Seattle company engaged in special trade contracting.

UNIVERSITY FEDERAL SAVINGS BANK
6400 Roosevelt Way North East, Seattle WA 98115. 206/526-1000. Contact Personnel Department. A key Seattle bank.

URS ENGINEERS
3131 Elliott Avenue, Suite 300, Seattle WA 98121. 206/284-3131. Contact John Cykler, Personnel Director. A major diversified professional service organization providing design, planning, and construction management services to clients in the public and private sectors. Areas of specialization include environmental research and preservation, energy, and water resources. Corporate headquarters location: San Mateo CA.

US WEST, NEW VECTOR GROUP
3350 161st, South East, Bellevue WA 98008. 206/747-4900. Contact Donna Ments, Personnel Department. A company specializing in cellular mobile commercial products and services.

VALLEY NEWSPAPERS
600 South Washington, P.O. Box 130, Kent WA 98035-0130. 206/872-6600. Contact Georgie Heath, Secretary. The publishers of the Daily Globe News, Auburn; Daily News Journal, Kent; and Daily Record Chronicle, Renton. Parent company: Donrey Media Group. Common positions include: Advertising Worker; Bookkeeper; Commercial Artist; Reporter/Editor. Company benefits include: medical, dental, and life insurance; pension plan; disability coverage. Corporate headquarters location: Fort Smith, AR.

VANCOUVER DIVISION/ HEWLETT PACKARD

P.O. Box C-006, Vancouver WA 98668-0006. Mailed inquiries only. Contact Personnel Department. A company which Produces workstation printers including serial impact and serial inkjet printers. Parent company, Hewlett Packard, is engaged in the design and manufacture of measurement and computation products and systems used in business, industry, engineering, science, health care, and education; principal products are integrated instrument and computer systems (including hardware and software), computer systems and peripheral products, and medical electronic equipment and systems.

VERNELL'S CANDY COMPANY

11959 Northup Way, Bellevue WA 98004. 206/455-8400. Contact Bill Osber, Personnel Department. A major Bellevue candy company.

VITA-MILK DAIRY, INC.

427 North East 72nd, Seattle WA 98115. 206/524-7070. Contact Contact Personnel Department. A key Seattle manufacturer of dairy products.

WADE & BRADY INTERNATIONAL, INC.

601 Valley Street, P.O. Box 9448, Seattle WA 98109. 206/282-6510. Contact Personnel Department. A key operator of non residential buildings in Seattle.

THE SEATTLE JOB BANK

WARDS COVE PACKING COMPANY, INC.
88 East Hamlin Street, Seattle WA 98102. 206/323-3200. Contact Personnel Department. A primary Seattle company engaged in salmon canneries and general retail.

WASHINGTON MORTGAGE CORPORATION
2720 Third Avenue, Suite 300, Seattle WA 98121. 206/441-6540. Contact Personnel Department. A prominent Seattle mortgage banker.

WASHINGTON MUTUAL
12360 Lake City Way NE, Seattle WA 98125. 206/367-0300. Contact Personnel Department. A leading Seattle bank.

WASHINGTON MUTUAL SAVINGS BANK
1101 2nd Avenue, Seattle WA 98101. 206/464-4400. Contact Personnel Department. A prominent Seattle bank.

WASHINGTON NATURAL GAS COMPANY
815 Mercer Street, Seattle WA 98111. 206/622-6767. Contact Personnel Department. A leading natural gas distributor of Seattle.

WASHINGTON STATE
DAIRY PRODUCTS COMMISSION
1107 North East 45th, Suite 205, Seattle WA 98105. 206/545-6763. Contact Personnel Department. A company engaged in the advertisement and promotion of milk and dairy product companies.

WASHINGTON STATE APPLE COMMISSION
P.O. Box 18, Wenatchee WA 98801. 509/663-9600. Contact Personnel Department. A company engaged in the advertisement and promotion of Washington State apples.

WASHINGTON STATE DEPARTMENT OF TRADE & ECONOMIC DEVELOPMENT, TOURISM DEV. DIV.
101 General Administration Building, Olympia WA 98504. 206/753-5600. Contact Personnel Department. A division of the state of Washington involved in tourism development and promotion.

WASHINGTON STATE POTATO COMMISSION
108 Interlake Road, Moses Lake WA 98837. 509/765-8845. Contact Personnel Department. A division in charge of Washington potatoes, fresh and processed.

THE WASHINGTON WATER POWER COMPANY
East 1411 Mission Avenue, Spokane WA 99202. 509/489-0500. Contact Personnel Department. A leading area utility supplying electric power and natural gas.

WEISFIELDS, INC.
800 South Michigan Street, Seattle WA 98108. 206/767-5011. Contact Personnel Department. A prime Seattle company engaged in the retail of jewelry.

WEST COAST GROCERY COMPANY
P.O. Box 2237, Tacoma WA 98401. 206/593-5876. Contact Employment Manager. A company engaged in wholesale grocery distribution.

WESTARS MOTOR COACHES, INC.
300 Elliott Avenue West, Seattle WA 98119. 206/281-3535. Contact Personnel Department. A primary Seattle motor coach transportation company.

WESTERN MARINE ELECTRONICS
P.O. Box C-3001, Bothell WA 98041-3001. 206/285-2420. Contact Susan Black, Personnel Director. A company which manufactures a variety of electronics equipment for diverse end uses; products include scanning and sonar equipment and related industrial measurement machinery.

WESTERN NATIONAL ASSURANCE, INC.
9706 4th Avenue North East, Seattle WA 98125. 206/526-5900. Contact Personnel Department. A leading Seattle insurance agents and brokers service company.

WESTERN PHOTOGRAPHICS, INC.
953 North 128th, Seattle WA 98133. 206/364-1070. Contact Personnel Department. A leading photography

THE SEATTLE JOB BANK

company engaged in photographic processing, enlargements, and related photographic access.

WESTERN UTILITIES SUPPLY COMPANY
5409 Ohio Avenue South, P.O. Box 3524, Seattle WA 98124. 206/762-7025. Contact Personnel Department. A prominent Seattle company engaged in the wholesale of industrial water works supplies. Common job positions include: Sales Representative. Principal educational backgrounds sought: Marketing. Company benefits include: medical insurance; dental insurance; pension plan; life insurance; tuition assistance; disability coverage. Corporate headquarters. Operations at this facility include: administration; service; sales.

WESTIN HOTEL COMPANY
2001 6th Avenue, Seattle WA 98121. Mailed inquiries only. Contact Walker Williams, Personnel Director. Operates a national chain of quality hotels. Corporate headquarters location.

WESTMARK INTERNATIONAL
Columbia Center, Suite 6800, 701 Fifth Avenue, Seattle WA 98104. 206/682-6800. Contact Personnel Department. A leading manufacturing company of medical supplies.

WESTMEDIA CORPORATION

770 11th Avenue, P.O. Box 189, Longview WA 98632. 206/577-2514. Contact Steve Lafady, Director of Human Resources. A company which publishes an area evening newspaper, the Daily News, with a circulation of over 25,000. Common positions include: Accountant; Administrator; Advertising Worker; Commercial Artist; Computer Programmer; Customer Service Representative; Department Manager; Operations/Production Manager; Marketing Specialist; Personnel & Labor Relations Specialist; Reporter/Editor; Sales Representative. Principal educational backgrounds sought: Accounting; Business Administration; Computer Science; Marketing; Journalism. Company benefits include: medical, dental and life insurance; pension plan; tuition assistance; disability coverage. Corporate headquarters location. Operations at this facility include: manufacturing; administration; sales.

★ WEYERHAEUSER COMPANY

College Relations & Recruiting, WTC-TR1, Tacoma WA 98477. Mailed inquiries only. Contact Personnel. Send resume with cover letter. One of the world's largest forest products companies. Products include lumber, plywood, pulp, shipping and milk cartons, specialty papers, and panel products. Also engaged in real estate development and the management of nurseries and ornamentals. Corporate headquarters location. Operations at this facility include: manufacturing; research/development; administration; service; sales. New York Stock Exchange. Common positions include: Accountant; Computer Programmer;

Economist; Engineer; Chemical Engineer; Electrical Engineer; Industrial Engineer; Mechanical Engineer; Financial Analyst; Forester; Management Trainee; Sales Representative. Principal educational backgrounds sought: Accounting; Biology; Computer Science; Engineering; Finance; Marketing. Company benefits include: medical insurance; dental insurance; pension plan; life insurance; tuition assistance; disability coverage.

WINMAR COMPANY, INC.
900 4th Avenue, Suite 800, Seattle WA 98111. 206/223-4500. Contact Personnel Department. A principal real estate developer and investment company.

WMC CONTRACTORS, INC.
13800 Pacific Highway South, Seattle WA 98168. 206/433-1600. Contact Personnel Department. A key Seattle piping and heating contractors company.

IS WOLFE & PARTNERS
119 Aloha Street, Seattle WA 98109. 206/282-9598. Contact Personnel Department. A prominent investment club

WOMEN'S AGLOW FELLOWSHIP
P.O. Box 1548, Lynwood WA 98046-1556. 206/775-7282. Contact Colleen Bronson, Personnel Director. An area publisher with activities in religious titles, as well as in other works.

WRIGHT HOWARDS CONSTRUCTION COMPANY
P.O. Box 3764, Seattle WA 98124. 206/447-7654. Contact Personnel Department. A principal Seattle general contracting company of non residential buildings other than industrial buildings and warehouses.

WRIGHT RUNSTAD & COMPANY
1201 3rd Avenue, Suite 2000, Seattle WA 98104. 206/447-9000. Contact Personnel Department. A primary Seattle commercial real estate developer.

WRIGHT SCHUCHART, INC.
425 Pontius Avenue North, Seattle WA 98109. 206/447-7545. Contact Dan McDougall, V.P./Human Resources Director. A holding company with subsidiary operations in commercial contracting.

WTB FINANCIAL CORPORATION
P.O. Box 2127, Spokane WA 99210. 509/455-4160. Contact Walker Collins, Treasurer. A holding company with subsidiary banking operations offering a wide range of financial services.

✴ XEROX CORPORATION
6400 South Center Boulevard, Tukwila WA 98188. 206/241-1388. Contact Sandy Dolan, Personnel Director. Nationally, the firm is a major worldwide manufacturer of business machines, copiers, computer systems, and word processors. Also publishes educational materials through various subsidiaries, and manufactures other products such as aerospace systems and components, electrostatic printers, microfiche

printers, and many other related products and services. In addition, the company provides international communications services and systems. Corporate headquarters location: Stamford, CT. New York Stock Exchange.

YAKIMA HERALD-REPUBLIC
P.O. Box 9668, Yakima WA 98909. 509/248-1251. Contact Kay Gause, Personnel Director. Publishes a local newspaper with a circulation of more than 35,000. A member of the Harte Hanks Communications Group.

YARBOROUGH & VESSEY
12319 Fourth Avenue South, 98168 WA 98168. 206/433-1011. Contact Personnel Department. A leading Seattle real estate and investment company.

ARTHUR YOUNG & COMPANY
#2200 One Union Square, Seattle WA 98101. 206/623-9000. Contact Bill Solomon, Personnel Director. Nationally, the firm is a major certified public accounting firm with operations in auditing and accounting, tax services, and management consulting. Company has approximately 5,000 professionals and 600 partners and directors in offices throughout the United States. Corporate headquarters location: New York, NY.

YUKSEL, INC.
3822 57th SW, Seattle WA 98116. 206/937-8119. Contact Personnel Department. A leading Seattle operator of apartment buildings.

ZELLERBACH PAPER COMPANY

6301 Airport Way, Seattle WA 98108. 206/383-1416. Contact Human Resources Manager. A company operating in 13 Western states, the firm offers a highly diversified product line including paper for commercial printers, industrial packaging supplies, films and foils for food processing, and agricultural packaging systems. A division of Crown-Zellerbach Company, but operates with its own company headquarters. Corporate headquarters location: San Francisco, CA.

ZYMOGENETICS, INC.

4225 Roosevelt Way North East, Seattle WA 98105. 206/547-8080. Contact Laura Robb, Personnel Manager. A Seattle subsidiary of Novo Industri of Denmark. A company involved in research directed at proteins of therapeutic value in wound repair and other areas. Common job positions include: Biochemist; Biologist; Financial Analyst. Principal educational backgrounds sought: Biology; Business Administration; Marketing; Biochemistry. Company benefits: medical insurance; dental insurance; life insurance; tuition assistance; disability coverage; profit sharing; vacation; sick leave; auto insurance. Corporate headquarters. Parent company Novo Industries.

Industry Cross-Index

ACCOUNTING

ARTHUR ANDERSEN & COMPANY
DELOITTE HASKINS & SELLS
PRICE WATERHOUSE
ARTHUR YOUNG & COMPANY

ADVERTISING

AMERICAN PASSAGE MEDIA CORPORATION
BORDERS, PERRIN & NORRANDER
BREMS EASTMAN
JOHN BROWN & PARTNERS
CEDARCREST ADVERTISING
CLARK/WHITE & ASSOCIATES
COLE & WEBER INC.
COONS, CORKER & ASSOCIATES
EHRIG & ASSOCIATES
ELGEE CORPORATION
ELGIN SYFERD
EVANS/KRAFT INC.
LIVINGSTON & COMPANY
McCANN-ERICKSON/SEATTLE
MOGELGAARD and ASSOCIATES
SANDILANDS WURZ HAFELI LOGES
SEA GALLEY RESTAURANTS
SHARP HARTWIG ADVERTISING
THE STIMPSON CLARK INC.
STRATEGIC DIRECT

THOMPSON RECRUITMENT ADVERTISING INC.
TYCER FULTZ BELLACK/DAVIS

ARTS AND RECREATION

EP INDUSTRIES, INC.
NACO-WEST INC.

APPAREL AND TEXTILES

JANTZEN INC.
PACIFIC TRAIL INC.
SEATTLE PACIFIC INDUSTRIES, INC.

BANKING/SAVINGS AND LOAN

BANK OF PUGET SOUND
FAMILY SAVINGS AND LOAN ASSOCIATION
FIRST INTERSTATE BANK OF WASHINGTON
GIBRALTAR SAVINGS OF WASHINGTON F.A.
GREAT WESTERN FEDERAL SAVINGS BANK
METROPOLITAN FEDERAL SAVINGS & LOAN
NORTHWEST BANK
PACIFIC FIRST FEDERAL SAVINGS BANK
SAVINGS BANK OF PUGET SOUND
SEAFIRST CORPORATION
SEATTLE - FIRST NATIONAL BANK
SEATTLE TRUST & SAVINGS BANK
U.S. BANK OF WASHINGTON
UNITED SAVINGS AND LOAN BANK

THE SEATTLE JOB BANK

UNIVERSITY FEDERAL SAVINGS BANK
WASHINGTON MUTUAL

BOOK AND MAGAZINE PUBLISHING

ALASKA NORTHWEST PUBLISHING COMPANY
MADRONA PUBLISHERS INC.
MOUNTAINEERS BOOKS
PEANUT BUTTER PUBLISHING
WOMEN'S AGLOW FELLOWSHIP

CHARITABLE, NON-PROFIT, AND HUMANITARIAN

TACOMA GOODWILL INDUSTRIES

CHEMICALS: PRODUCTION, PROCESSING

AUTO CHLOR SYSTEM OF WASHINGTON, B01
BARDAHL MANUFACTURING CORPORATION
GACO WESTERN INC.
GRAYS HARBOR DIVISION
OLYMPIC HOMECARE PRODUCTS COMPANY
PRESERVATIVE PAINT COMPANY
UNIVAR CORPORATION

COMMUNICATIONS

ACKERLY COMMUNICATIONS INC.

THE SEATTLE JOB BANK

ANIXTER-SEATTLE
ATTACHMATE CORPORATION
AUGAT COMMUNICATIONS
GENERAL TELEPHONE COMPANY
HONEYWELL INC.
IBM CORPORATION
IGM COMMUNICATIONS
LAKE STEVENS INSTRUMENT DIVISION
MUZAK
NCR CORPORATION
NORTHLAND CABLE PROPERTIES FOUR LTD.
PACIFIC NORTHWEST BELL
PACIFIC TELECOM INC.
PROCTOR & ASSOCIATES COMPANY
SPOKANE DIVISION
SQUARE D COMPANY
TELTONE CORPORATION
TONE COMMANDER SYSTEMS INC.

COMPUTER-RELATED: HARDWARE, SOFTWARE, AND SERVICES

BOEING COMPUTER SERVICE COMPANY
DP ENTERPRISES, INC.
DATA I/O CORPORATION
KEY TRONIC CORPORATION
MANNESMANN TALLY CORPORATION
MICROSOFT CORPORATION
XEROX CORPORATION

THE SEATTLE JOB BANK

CONSTRUCTION: MATERIALS AND SERVICES

AMERICAN PLYWOOD ASSOCIATION
BAUGH CONSTRUCTION COMPANY
ROBERT E. BAYLEY CONSTRUCTION
BAYLINER MARINE CORPORATION
BROWN GORDON INC.
CAPITAL DEVELOPMENT COMPANY
CHRISTENSON RABER KIEF ASSOC.
FENTRON BUILDING PRODUCTS INC.
JAMES PAUL JONES
KNIK CONSTRUCTION COMPANY INC.
MANSON CONSTRUCTION ENGINEERING COMPANY
MEHRER DRYWALL INC.
MWK INTERNATIONAL LTD INC.
PACIFIC COAST FEATHER COMPANY INC.
PRIME CONSTRUCTION COMPANY INC.
SHAKERTOWN CORPORATION
THE SIMPSON DOOR COMPANY
UNIFLITE, INC.
UNIVERSAL SERVICES INC.-INTERNATIONAL

DEFENSE AND GOVERNMENT RELATED

CRITON TECHNOLOGIES
OLIN DEFENSE SYSTEMS GROUP
ROCKCOR INC.

ELECTRONICS

ADVANCED TECHNOLOGY LABORATORIES INC.
AMERICAN SIGN AND INDICATOR CORPORATION
APPLIED MICROSYSTEMS CORPORATION
AUDIO GROUP INC.
AVTECH CORPORATION
BELL INDUSTRIES
COCHRAN ELECTRIC COMPANY INC.
CX CORPORATION
DATACOM NORTHWEST INC.
ELDEC CORPORATION
ESTERLINE CORPORATION
HEWLETT PACKARD COMPANY
INTEGRATED CIRCUITS INC.
JOHN FLUKE MANUFACTURING COMPANY, INC.
KEY TRONIC CORPORATION
KORRY ELECTRONICS
MANNESMAN-TALLY CORPORATION
OPCON INC.
PACIFIC ELECTRO DYNAMICS
PHSIO-CONTROL CORPORATION
QUINTON INSTRUMENTS COMPANY
RATELCO INC.
SCA WOLFF SYSTEM
SUNDSTRAND DATA CONTROL, INC.
TAPCO
US WEST, NEW VECTOR GROUP
WESTERN MARINE ELECTRONICS

ENGINEERING

ABAM ENGINEERS INC.
RW BECK & ASSOCIATES
BOVAY ENGINEERS INC.
BUSINESS SPACE DESIGN
EDAW INC.
LANCE MUELLER & ASSOCIATES
NBBJ GROUP
PARSONS BRINCKERHOFF
STEPAN & ASSOCIATES
URS ENGINEERS

FABRICATED METALS

ALASKAN COPPER WORKS
ATLAS FOUNDRY & MACHINE COMPANY
CAPITAL INDUSTRIES INC.
COLUMBIA MACHINE INC.
GOLUB SIMON & SONS INC.
INTALCO ALUMINUM CORPORATION
JORGENSEN STEEL
KAISER ALUMINUM & CHEMICAL CORPORATION
SEATTLE STEEL

FINANCIAL SERVICES

AP DEVELOPMENT INC.

THE SEATTLE JOB BANK

BENAROYA SECURITIES COMPANY
BROWN AND CALDWELL
CABLE HOUSE & RAGEN
CN DATA PROCESSING
FOSTER & MARSHALL
JOHN GRAHAM & COMPANY
INTERPACIFIC INVESTORS SERVICES
KEY BANK OF PUGET SOUND
LYDEN INC.
MANAGEMENT AND PLANNING SERVICES
MANUFACTURERS HANOVER
MARKET FINANCE COMPANY
OLD NATIONAL BANCORP
OLD STONE BANK OF WASHINGTON
OLYMPIC CAPITAL MANAGEMENT
PACIFIC FIRST FEDERAL
PEOPLES NATIONAL BANK OF WASHINGTON
PIERRE ENTERPRISES INC.
PUGET SOUND BANCORP
RAINIER NATIONAL BANK
SEA FIRST MORTGAGE CORPORATION
SEAFIRST CORPORATION
SEATTLE NORTHWEST SECURITY CORPORATION
SHANNON & WILSON
SIMPSON INVESTMENT COMPANY
SPRAGUE RESOURCES CORPORATION
UNIGARD SERVICE CORPORATION
TAMS CONSULTANTS
WASHINGTON MORTGAGE CORPORATION
I.S. WOLFE & PARTNERS
WRIGHT SCHUCHART INC.
WTB FINANCIAL CORPORATION

FOOD: DISTRIBUTION, PRODUCTION, AND PROCESSING

ACME POULTRY COMPANY INC.
ALASKA PACIFIC FISHERIES INC.
BARDIN FARMS CORPORATION
BERING ENTERPRISES LTD. PARTNERSHIP
CARNATION COMPANY
CHEF REDDY FOODS CORPORATION
CHUGACH AK FISHERIES INC.
CONTINENTAL BAKING COMPANY
CRESCENT MANUFACTURING COMPANY
DAIRY EXPORT COMPANY INC.
DAIRYGOLD, INC.
DEL MONTE CORPORATION
FARWEST SEAFOODS, INC.
FOOD SERVICES OF AMERICA
GAI'S SEATTLE FRENCH BAKING COMPANY
GENERAL BREWING CORPORATION
GREEN GIANT COMPANY/DAYTON PLANT
H&N INC.
HYGRADE FOOD PRODUCTS CORPORATION
ICICLE SEAFOODS INC.
LANGENDORF BAKING COMPANY OF SEATTLE
LIBERTY ORCHARDS COMPANY, INCORPORATED
MERLINO'S MACARONI, INCORPORATED
NALLEY'S FINE FOODS
OROWEAT BAKERS
PABST BREWING COMPANY/TUMWATER DIVISION

PETER PAN SEAFOODS INC.
RAINIER BANCORP
RAINIER BREWING COMPANY
ROMAN MEAL COMPANY
SNOKIST GROWERS
SOUTHLAND CORPORATION
SPECIALTY FOODS INTERNATIONAL
STADELMAN FRUIT INC.
P.J. TAGGARES COMPANY
TREE TOP INC.
TWIN CITY FOODS INC.
UI GROUP INC.
UNISEA
VERNELL'S CANDY COMPANY
VITA-MILK DAIRY INC.
WARDS COVE PACKING COMPANY INC.
WASHINGTON STATE POTATO COMMISSION

FOOD/TRADE

CURTICE BURNS FOODS
FOOD GIANT STORES
NORTHWEST DAIRYMENS ASSOCIATION
PETER PAN SEAFOODS, INC.
ROSAVER'S SUPERMARKETS
SEATTLE MARINE FISHING SUPPLY COMPANY
THRIFTY FOODS INC.
TRADEWELL STORES INC.
KEITH UDDENBERG INC.
WASHINGTON STATE APPLE COMMISSION
WEST COAST GROCERY COMPANY

GENERAL MERCHANDISE/TRADE

ASSOCIATED GROCERS INC.
EDDIE BAUER INC.
THE BON
BRANOM INSTRUMENT COMPANY
BEN BRIDGE CORPORATION
CENTURY 21 PROMOTIONS INC.
WILLIAM B. CLOES
THE CRESCENT
EGGHEAD INCORPORATED
FIRST CITY CREDIT
FISHERIES SUPPLY COMPANY
FOSS LAUNCH & TUG COMPANY
FOXS GEMSHOP INC.
GEM EAST CORP.
GM NAMEPLATE INC.
JAY JACOBS INC.
JENSEN-BYRD COMPANY INC.
K-MART STORES
K2 CORPORATION
MAGNOLIA HI-FI INC.
NORDSTROM INC.
NORTHWEST FISHERIES ASSOCIATION
PACIFIC TRAIL SPORTSWEAR
PAY 'N PAC STORES INC.
PAYN SAVE INC.
PNS INC.
RECREATIONAL EUIPMENT INC.
ROFFE INC. D/B/A ROFFEE
SPORTCASTER COMPANY
WEISFIELDS INC.

HEALTH CARE AND PHARMACEUTICALS: PRODUCTS AND SERVICES

BIDDLE & CROWTHER COMPANY
EVERYLIFE NUTRITIONALS, INC.
IMMUNEX CORPORATION
IMRE CORPORATION
NORTHWESTERN DRUG COMPANY
PHYSIO-CONTROL CORPORATION
SPACELABS, INC.
WESTMARK INTERNATIONAL

HOTEL AND RESTAURANT RELATED

DENNY'S RESTAURANTS
HOAGY'S CORNER RESTAURANTS
PACIFIC INTERNATIONAL CORPORATION
PIZZA HAVEN INC.
RESTAURANTS UNLIMITED, INC.
SEA GALLEY STORES INC.
SKIPPER'S INCORPORATED
UNIVERSAL SERVICES INC.
WESTIN HOTELS & RESORTS

INSURANCE

AETNA LIFE & CASUALTY
AGENA CORPORATION
ALLSTATE SEATTLE

BLUE CROSS OF WASHINGTON AND ALASKA
CORROON & BLACK INC.
FAMILY LIFE INSURANCE COMPANY
FARMERS NEW WORLD LIFE INSURANCE COMPANY
FEDERATED AMERICAN INSURANCE COMPANY
FIREMAN'S FUND INSURANCE COMPANY
FIRST NATIONAL INSURANCE CO. OF AMERICA
GENERAL INSURANCE COMPANY OF AMERICA
GRANGE INSURANCE
GREAT REPUBLIC LIFE INSURANCE
MARSH & McLENNAN
NATIONAL MERIT INSURANCE COMPANY
NORTHERN LIFE INSURANCE COMPANY
PRUDENTIAL INSURANCE COMPANY OF AMERICA
PUBLIC EMPLOYEES MUTUAL INSURANCE
SAFECO CORPORATION
TRANSAMERICA TITLE INSURANCE
TRAVELERS INSURANCE COMPANY
UNIGARD INC.
UNIGARD INDEMMITY COMPANY INC.
UNIGARD INSURANCE COMPANY
UNITED PACIFIC INSURANCE
WESTERN NATIONAL ASSURANCE INC.

MANUFACTURING: MISCELLANEOUS CONSUMER

LANOGA COROPORATION
NINTENDO OF AMERICA
PRECOR U.S.A., INC.
RALEIGH CYCLE COMPANY OF AMERICA
SKYWAY LUGGAGE COMPANY
THAW CORPORATION

MANUFACTURING: MISCELLANEOUS INDUSTRIAL

AIMSCO INCORPORATED
E.J. BARTELLS COMPANY
BELSHAW BROTHER, INC.
COLUMBIA LIGHTING INC.
CONCRETE TECHNOLOGY CORPORATION
CONTINENTAL EMSCO COMPANY
HEMPHILL BROTHERS INC.
KENWORTH TRUCK COMPANY, PACCAR INC.
KEY INDUSTRIES INC.
LANOGA COROPORATION
PALMER G. LEWIS CO., INC.
MARCO SEATTLE
MARINE POWER & EQUIPMENT COMPANY, INC.
MODULINE INTERNATIONAL INC.
NORTH STAR ICE EQUIPMENT CORPORATION
PAINE CORPORATION
ROCKET RESEARCH COMPANY

ROHR BACK CORPORATION
SIGMA RESEARCH INC.
TEMPRESS INC.
VANCOUVER DIVISION
ZELLERBACH PAPER COMPANY

MISCELLANEOUS SERVICES

MILLIMAN & ROBERTSON INC.
NORTHWEST PROTECTIVE SERVICE INC.
TELLER TRAINING INSTITUTES, INC.
WESTERN PHOTOGRAPHICS, INC.

NEWSPAPER PUBLISHING

BELLINGHAM HERALD
THE BREMERTON SUN
COLUMBIA BASIN HERALD
THE COLUMBIAN NEWSPAPER
THE DAILY CHRONICLE
THE DAILY NEWS
DAILY RECORD
THE DAILY WORLD
THE HERALD
JOURNAL-AMERICAN
NEWS-TRIBUNE & LEDGER
THE OLYMPIAN
PENINSULA DAILY NEWS
SEATTLE DAILY JOURNAL OF COMMERCE
SEATTLE POST - INTELLIGENCER
SEATTLE TIMES COMPANY

SKAGIT VALLEY HERALD
THE SPOKESMAN-REVIEW & SPOKANE CHRONICLE
SUNNYSIDE DAILY NEWS
TACOMA NEWS TRIBUNE
TRI-CITY HERALD
TRIBUNE PUBLISHING COMPANY
VALLEY NEWSPAPERS
WESTMEDIA CORPORATION
YAKIMA HERALD-REPUBLIC

PAPER, PACKAGING AND FOREST PRODUCTS/CONTAINERS & GLASS PRODUCTS

ACRO-WOOD
BRAZIER FOREST INDUSTRIES INC.
BUFFELEN WOODWORKING COMPANY
CAMAS MILL DIVISION
CONTAINER CORPORATION OF AMERICA
DAISHOWA AMERICA COMPANY LTD.
IMAGES WOODWORKING, INC.
JAMES RIVER CORPORATION
KAVILCO INC.
KINNEAR OF WASHINGTON
LINDAL CEDAR HOMES INC.
LONGVIEW FIBRE COMPANY
MANKE LUMBER COMPANY INC.
MAYR BROTHERS LOGGING COMPANY INC.
MERRILL & RING INC.
NORTHWEST TIMBER DIVISION
NORTHWESTERN GLASS
PENINSULA PLYWOOD

PLUM CREEEK TIMBER COMPANY, INC.
RED CEDAR SHINGLE & HAND-SPLIT
SCOTT PAPER COMPANY
SIMPSON INVESTMENT COMPANY
SIMPSON TIMBER COMPANY
SKOWL ARM TIMBER CORPORATION
STEVENSON CO-PLY INC.
WEYERHAEUSER COMPANY

PETROLEUM AND ENERGY RELATED/MINING AND DRILLING

ARCO PETROLEUM PRODUCTS
ATLANTIC RICHFIELD COMPANY
BURLINGTON NORTHERN INC.
CASCADE NATURAL GAS CORPORATION
COMINCO AMERICAN INC.
KIEWITT INDUSTRIAL COMPANY
MOBIL OIL CORPORATION
TIME OIL COMPANY
WASHINGTON NATURAL GAS COMPANY
WMC CONTRACTORS INC.

PRINTING

CRAFTSMAN PRESS INC.
HAGGEN COMPANY
INTERMEC CORPORATION
UNITED GRAPHICS INC.

REAL ESTATE

ALEXANDER & VENTURA
BELL-ANDERSON REALTY INC.
BRYN MAWR PROPERTIES
COLDWELL BANKER
CUSHMAN & WAKEFIELD OF WASHINGTON INC.
FIRST CITY INVESTMENTS INC.
FIRST REAL ESTATE SALES INC.
FISCHER DIAC DEVELOPMENT INC.
GAN ENTERPRISES INC.
GLACIER PARK COMPANY
GREENWOOD ENTERPRISES
MAC PHERSONS INC.
MAC-RENT INC.
MASON PROPERTIES
THE NEWTON COMPANY
NEYHART COMPANY
NORTHGATE CENTERS
PETS INC.
PRESTON RIDGE FINANCIAL SERVICES CORP.
SAFECARE COMPANY INC.
SELLEN CONSTRUCTION COMPANY INC.
WADE & BRADY INTERNATIONAL INC.
WINMAR COMPANY INC.
WRIGHT HOWARDS CONSTRUCTION COMPANY
WRIGHT RUNSTAD & COMPANY
YARBOROUGH & VESSEY
YUKSEL INC.

RESEARCH AND DEVELOPMENT

CALLISON PARTNERSHIP LTD.
FACTORY MUTUAL ENGINEERING AND RESEARCH
ZYMOGENETICS, INC.

TRANSPORTATION

AIR VAN LINES
AIRBORNE FREIGHT CORPORATION
ALASKA AIRLINES, INC.
ANGEL LEE INC.
BEKINS MOVING & STORAGE COMPANY
BOEING AEROSPACE COMPANY
THE BOEING COMPANY
CONSOLIDATED FREIGHTWAYS
CONTINENTAL VAN LINES INC.
DOWTY DECOTO INC.
EAGLE MARINE SERVICES LTD.
ENGINEERING DEVELOPMENT CORPORATION
EXPEDITORS INTERNATIONAL OF WASHINGTON
EZ LOADER BOAT TRAILERS INC.
FIRESTONE TIRE & RUBBER COMPANY
FLIGHTCRAFT
FREMONT ELECTRIC COMPANY
HEATH TECNA AEROSPACE COMPANY
HOLLAND AMERICAN LINE - WESTOURS INC.
HORIZON AIR INDUSTRIES
INCO EXPRESS INC.

THE SEATTLE JOB BANK

INTERSTATE DISTRIBUTOR COMPANY
KENWORTH TRUCK COMPANY
MURRAY CHRISCRAFT WEST
NORTHERN AIR FREIGHT, INC.
OLD STONE CAPITAL CORPORATION
OLYMPIC SALES INC.
PACCAR INC.
PALMER GROUP
PRINCESS TOURS
PUGET SOUND FREIGHT LINES INC.
SCHUCK'S AUTO SUPPLY
SEA-LAND SERVICE INC.
SHELL OIL COMPANY
SHEPARD AMBULANCE, INC.
SOUTHWOOD MANOR
SUNDSTRAND DATA CONTROL INC.
SUNRISE RESORT & RECREATION
TACOMA BOATBUILDING COMPANY
TENNYS TOYOTA INC.
THAI AIRWAYS INTERNATIONAL, LTD.
TODD PACIFIC SHIPYARDS CORPORATION
TOLLYCRAFT YACHTS CORPORATION
UNIMAR
WESTARS MOTOR COACHES INC.

UTILITIES

PUGET SOUND POWER & LIGHT COMPANY
SEATTLE CITY LIGHT
THE WASHINGTON WATER POWER COMPANY
WESTERN UTILITIES SUPPLY COMPANY

Professional Employment Services

EMPLOYMENT AGENCIES AND TEMPORARY SERVICES OF WASHINGTON

ABLE PERSONNEL SERVICE
N4407 Division, Suite 625, Spokane, WA 99207. Contact William "Jay" Kinzer, Owner/Manager. (509) 487-2734. Employment agency. No appointment required. Founded 1964. Specializes in the areas of: Accounting and Finance; Clerical; Engineering; Sales and Marketing. Positions commonly filled include: Accountant; Administrative Assistant; Bookkeeper; Buyer; Claim Representative; Clerk; Credit Manager; Customer Service Representative; Data Entry Clerk; Draftsperson; General Manager; Legal Secretary; Marketing Specialist; Medical Secretary; Office Worker; Purchasing Agent; Receptionist; Sales Representative; Secretary; Stenographer; Typist; Word Processing Specialist. Individual pays fee.

A.S.A.P. EMPLOYMENT SERVICES
4171 Wheaton Way, Suite 7, Bremerton, WA 98310. Contact Roberta I. Long, Owner. (206) 479-4310. Employment agency; temporary help service. Appointment requested. Founded 1973. Nonspecialized. Positions commonly filled include: Accountant; Administrative Assistant; Advertising Worker; Bank Officer/Manager; Bookkeeper; Buyer; Civil Engineer; Claim Representative; Clerk; Computer Operator; Computer Programmer; Credit Manager; Customer Service Representative; Data Entry Clerk;

Demonstrator; Draftsperson; EDP Specialist; Electrical Engineer; General Manager; Hotel Manager; Legal Secretary; Industrial Engineer; Mechanical Engineer; Medical Secretary; Nurse; Office Worker; Public Relations Worker; Purchasing Agent; Quality Control Supervisor; Receptionist; Reporter/Editor; Sales Representative; Secretary; Stenographer; Systems Analyst; Technical Writer/Editor; Technician; Word Processing Specialist. Company pays fee; individual pays fee. Number of placements per year: 201-500.

CAREER SERVICES
1515 George Washington Way, Suite B, Richland, WA 99352. Contact J. B. McKee, Owner. (509) 946-0643. Employment agency; temporary help service. Appointment requested. Founded 1974. Specializes in the areas of: Accounting and Finance; Advertising; Banking; Bilingual; Clerical; Computer Hardware and Software; Engineering; Health and Medical; Insurance; Legal; MIS/EDP; Minorities; Personnel and Human Resources; Printing and Publishing; Sales and Marketing; Technical and Scientific. Positions commonly filled include: Accountant; Administrative Assistant; Advertising Worker; Agricultural Engineer; Architect; Attorney; Bank Officer/Manager; Biomedical Engineer; Bookkeeper; Buyer; Ceramics Engineer; Chemical Engineer; Chemist; Civil Engineer; Claim Representative; Clerk; Commercial Artist; Computer Operator; Computer Programmer; Credit Manager; Customer Service Representative; Data Entry Clerk; Demonstrator; Dietician; Draftsperson; Driver; EDP Specialist; Electrical Engineer; Financial Analyst;

Food Technologist; General Manager; Hotel Manager/Assistant Manager; Industrial Engineer; Insurance Agent/Broker; Legal Secretary; Light Industrial Worker; MIS Specialist; Marketing Specialist; Mechanical Engineer; Medical Secretary; Metallurgical Engineer; Model; Nurse; Office Worker; Operations/Production Specialist; Personnel and Labor Relations Specialist; Public Relations Worker; Purchasing Agent; Quality Control Supervisor; Receptionist; Reporter/Editor; Sales Representative; Secretary; Statistician; Stenographer; Systems Analyst; Technical Writer/Editor; Technician; Typist; Underwriter; Word Processing Specialist. Company pays fee; individual pays fee. Number of placements per year: 101-200.

FERREE & ASSOC. INC.
Post Office Box 3977, Federal Way, WA 98063-3977. Contact Thomas Ferree, President. (206) 941-4950. Employment agency. Appointment required. Founded 1978. Specializes in the Hotel/Resort/Country Club industry. Professionally staffed research department. Company tracks 1100+ hotel companies, 10,000+ hotels/resorts/conference centers and 2000+ clubs. Salaries $20,000-200,000+. Company pays fee. Number of placements per year: 51-100.

GILMORE TEMPORARY PERSONNEL
2722 Colby, Suite 506, Everett, WA 98201. Contact Colleen Ellingson, Manager. (206) 252-1195. Temporary help service. Appointment requested.

Founded 1969. Nonspecialized. Positions commonly filled include: Administrative Assistant; Bookkeeper; Clerk; Computer Operator; Data Entry Clerk; Demonstrator; Factory Worker; Legal Secretary; Light Industrial Worker; Medical Secretary; Office Worker; Receptionist; Secretary; Statistician; Stenographer; Typist; Word Processing Specialist. Company pays fee. Number of placements per year: 1001+.

HALLMARK SERVICES
217 Pine Street, Suite 510, Seattle, WA 98101. Contact David Waterbury, C.P.C., President. (206) 587-5360. Employment agency; temporary help service. No appointment required. Founded 1981. Specializes in the areas of: Clerical; Legal. Positions commonly filled include: Administrative Assistant; Bookkeeper; Clerk; Data Entry Clerk; Demonstrator; Office Worker; Receptionist; Secretary; Stenographer; Typist; Word Processing Specialist. Company pays fee; individual pays fee.

HOUSER, MARTIN, MORRIS & ASSOCIATES
110 110th Avenue, North West, Post Office Box C-90015, Bellevue, WA 98009. Contact David Martin, President. (206) 453-2700. Employment agency. Appointment requested. Founded 1974. Specializes in the areas of: Accounting and Finance; Banking; Computer Hardware and Software; Engineering; Insurance; Manufacturing; MIS/EDP; Sales and Marketing. Positions commonly filled include: Accountant; Actuary; Aerospace Engineer; Bank

Officer/Manager; Computer Programmer; Credit Manager; EDP Specialist; Electrical Engineer; Financial Analyst; General Manager; Industrial Engineer; Insurance Agent/Broker; MIS Specialist; Mechanical Engineer; Metallurgical Engineer; Purchasing Agent; Underwriter. Company pays fee.

JOBS CO.
East 8900 Sprague Avenue, Spokane, WA 99212. Contact Clark E. Hager, Sr., Owner. (509) 928-3151. Employment agency. Appointment required. Founded 1973. Largest agency in Spokane - nationwide professional placement and search. Includes Med/Search, Pro/Search, Sales/Search, and EDP/Search divisions. Specializes in the areas of: Accounting; Banking and Finance; Computer Hardware and Software; Engineering; Health and Medical; Manufacturing; MIS/EDP; Sales and Marketing; Secretarial and Clerical; Technical and Scientific. Positions commonly filled include: Accountant; Administrative Assistant; Aerospace Engineer; Agricultural Engineer; Bank Officer/Manager; Biochemist/Chemist; Biomedical Engineer; Civil Engineer; Computer Programmer; Dietician/Nutritionist; EDP Specialist; Electrical Engineer; Executive Secretary; Financial Analyst; Industrial Designer; Industrial Engineer; Legal Secretary; Management Consultant; Mechanical Engineer; Medical Secretary; Metallurgical Engineer; Mining Engineer; Nurse; Personnel Director; Petroleum; Physicist; Receptionist; Sales Representative; Secretary; Stenographer; Systems

Analyst; Typist; Word Processor. Company pays fee. Number of placements per year: 501-1000.

PERSONNEL UNLIMITED INC.
West 1528 Sharp Spokane, WA 99201. Contact Charlie Keturakat, Vice President. (509) 326-8880. Employment agency. Appointment requested. Founded 1978. Specializes in the areas of: Accounting and Finance; Clerical; Computer Hardware and Software; Engineering; Food Industry; Health and Medical; Insurance; Legal; MIS/EDP; Sales and Marketing. Positions commonly filled include: Accountant; Administrative Assistant; Agricultural Engineer; Bank Officer/Manager; Bookkeeper; Buyer; Claim Representative; Clerk; Computer Operator; Computer Programmer; Credit Manager; Customer Service Representative; Data Entry Clerk; Draftsperson; EDP Specialist; Electrical Engineer; Financial Analyst; General Manager; Hotel Manager/Assistant Manager; Industrial Engineer; Legal Secretary; MIS Specialist; Marketing Specialist; Mechanical Engineer; Medical Secretary; Metallurgical Engineer; Office Worker; Operations/Production Specialist; Public Relations Worker; Purchasing Agent; Quality Control Supervisor; Receptionist; Sales Representative; Secretary; Statistician; Stenographer; Systems Analyst; Technical Writer/Editor; Technician; Typist; Underwriter; Word Processing Specialist. Company pays fee; individual pays fee. Number of placements per year: 501-1000.

RAINIER HOME HEALTH CARE

1530 South Union, Suite 10, Tacoma, WA 98405. Contact Barbara Minick, Business Manager. (206) 759-8060. Appointment required. Founded 1971. Full service Medicare/Medicaid provider. Services include: RN, PT, OT, ST, MSW, HHA. Private program includes RN, LPN, HHA and Homehelper services 2-24 hours/day, seven days/week. Positions commonly filled include: Accountant; Administrative Assistant; Bookkeeper; Data Entry Clerk; Dietician/Nutritionist; Medical Secretary; Nurse; Public Relations Worker; Typist, etc. Individual pays fee. Number of placements per year: 51-100.

SNELLING & SNELLING OF SEATTLE

131 South West 153rd Post Office Box 66552, Seattle, WA 98166. Contact Jo Mabin Peterson, Owner/Manager. (206)246-6610. Employment agency. Appointment requested. Founded 1966. Specializes in the areas of: Banking; Clerical; Insurance; Retail Management; Sales and Marketing. Positions commonly filled include: Accountant; Administrative Assistant; Bank Officer/Manager; Bookkeeper; Claim Representative; Advertising Worker; Clerk; Computer Operator; Credit Manager; Customer Service Representative; Data Entry Clerk; Financial Analyst; Insurance Agent/Broker; Legal Secretary; Medical Secretary; Office Worker; Receptionist; Sales Representative; Secretary; Stenographer; Typist; Underwriter; Word Processing Specialist. Company pays fee; individual pays fee. Number of placements per year: 201-500.

STAFF BUILDERS, INC. OF WASHINGTON

10740 Meridian Avenue North Seattle, WA 98133. (206) 364-0535 or (206) 572-3455. Temporary help service. Appointment requested. Founded 1961. Branch offices located in: Arizona; California; Connecticut; District of Columbia; Florida; Georgia; Illinois; Indiana; Kansas; Louisiana; Maryland; Massachusetts; Michigan; Minnesota; Missouri; Nevada; New Jersey; New Mexico; New York; Ohio; Oklahoma; Oregon; Pennsylvania; Rhode Island; Tennessee; Texas; Virginia; Washington. Nonspecialized. Positions commonly filled include: Accountant; Administrative Assistant; Bookkeeper; Clerk; Companion; Computer Operator; Computer Programmer; Customer Service Representative; Data Entry Clerk; Demonstrator; Draftsperson; Driver; EDP Specialist; Factory Worker; General Laborer; Health Aide; Legal Secretary; Light Industrial Worker; Medical Secretary; Nurse; Office Worker; Public Relations Worker; Receptionist; Sales Representative; Secretary; Stenographer; Technician; Typist; Word Processing Specialist. Company pays fee. Number of placements per year: 1001+.

THE THOMAS COMPANY

Post Office Box 58155, Renton, WA 98058. Contact Thomas J. Yankowski, F.L.M.I., Executive Director. (206) 255-7637. Employment agency. Appointment required. Founded 1979. Nationwide search firm specializing in the Insurance industry. Specializes in the areas of: Banking and Finance; Computer Hardware and Software; Insurance; MIS/EDP; Sales and Marketing. Positions commonly filled include: Accountant; Actuary; Administrative Assistant; Advertising Executive; Attorney; Bookkeeper; Claims Representative; Computer Programmer; Customer Service Rep; Data Entry Clerk; EDP Specialist; Economist; Financial Analyst; General Manager. Insurance Agent/Broker; Management Consultant; Marketing Specialist; Personnel Director; Statistician; Systems Analyst; Technical Writer/Editor; Technician; Underwriter, etc. Company pays fee. Number of placements per year: 51-100.

VESTA CUTTING ASSOCIATES

1218 Third Avenue, Seattle Towers, Suite 817, Seattle, WA 98101. Contact Evelyn McKenzie Chase or Carolyn Aiken, Partners. (206) 622-3480. Employment agency. No appointment required. Founded 1948. Specializes in the areas of: Accounting and Finance; Banking; Clerical; Construction; Legal. Positions commonly filled include: Accountant; Administrative Assistant; Bookkeeper; Buyer; Claim Representative; Clerk; Computer Operator; Credit Manager; Customer Service Representative; Data Entry Clerk; EDP Specialist; Legal Secretary; Medical Secretary; Office Worker; Purchasing Agent; Receptionist; Secretary; Stenographer; Typist; Underwriter; Word Processing Specialist. Company pays fee. Number of placements per year: 51-100.

THE SEATTLE JOB BANK

EXECUTIVE SEARCH FIRMS OF WASHINGTON

COMPUSEARCH OF SEATTLE
2510 Fairview Avenue, East Post Office Box 12066, Seattle, WA 98102. Contact Dan Jilka, General Manager, or Jim Hayes, Manager. (206) 328-0936; FAX (206) 328-7221. Executive search firm. Appointment required; no phone calls; unsolicited resumes accepted. Founded 1965. World's largest contingency search firm. Five hundred offices nationwide, doing business under the names "Management Recruiters", "Sales Consultants", "CompuSearch" and "OfficeMates5". Specializes in mid-management/professional positions, $25,000-75,000. Specializes in the areas of: Accounting; Administration, MIS/EDP; Advertising; Affirmative Action; Architecture; Banking and Finance; Communications; Computer Hardware and Software; Construction; Electrical; Engineering; Food Industry; General Management; Health and Medical; Human Resources; Industrial and Interior Design; Insurance; Legal; Manufacturing; Operations Management; Printing and Publishing; Procurement; Real Estate; Retailing; Sales and Marketing; Technical and Scientific; Textiles; Transportation. Contingency.

COMPUSEARCH OF TACOMA
The Washington Building, Suite 806, 1019 Pacific Avenue Tacoma, WA 98402. Contact Ron Westover, General Manager, or Donn Dore, Manager. (206) 627-1972. Executive search firm. Appointment required; no

phone calls; unsolicited resumes accepted. Founded 1965. World's largest contingency search firm. Five hundred offices nationwide, doing business under the names "Management Recruiters", "Sales Consultants", "CompuSearch" and "OfficeMates5". Specializes in mid-management/professional positions, $25,000-75,000. Specializes in the areas of: Accounting; Administration, MIS/EDP; Advertising; Affirmative Action; Architecture; Banking and Finance; Communications; Computer Hardware and Software; Construction; Electrical; Engineering; Food Industry; General Management; Health and Medical; Human Resources; Industrial and Interior Design; Insurance; Legal; Manufacturing; Operations Management; Printing and Publishing; Procurement; Real Estate; Retailing; Sales and Marketing; Technical and Scientific; Textiles; Transportation. Contingency.

COX & ASSOCIATES

740 14th Avenue West Kirkland, WA 98033. Contact Charlene Cox, President. (206) 827-1670. Executive search firm. Appointment requested; unsolicited resumes accepted. Founded 1981. Specializes in the areas of: Aerospace; Computer Hardware and Software; Engineering; Technical and Scientific; Contingency; noncontingency. Number of searches conducted per year: 51-100.

EXECUTIVE SEARCH

West 1528 Sharp Spokane, WA 99201. Contact Gary Desgrosellier, President. (509) 326-8880. Executive search firm. Appointment requested; unsolicited resumes accepted. Founded 1981. Specializes in the areas of: Accounting; Administration MIS/EDP; Computer Hardware and Software; Engineering; Finance; Health and Medical; Insurance; Legal; Sales and Marketing. Contingency. Number of searches conducted per year: 51-100.

KATHY EVANS EXECUTIVE SEARCH, INC.
400 108th North East, #310 Bellevue, WA 98004. Contact Kathy Evans, President. (206) 453-5548. Executive search firm. Appointment required. Founded 1980. Specializes in the areas of: Health and Medical; Sales and Marketing. Positions commonly filled include: Sales Representative. Company pays fee. Number of placements per year: 0-50.

THE KNAPP AGENCY
1011 Securities Building Seattle, WA 98101. Contact Odessa F. Frost, Owner. (206) 623-2323. Executive search firm. Appointment requested; unsolicited resumes accepted. Founded 1955. Nonspecialized. Contingency; noncontingency. Number of searches conducted per year: 51-100.

MANAGEMENT RECRUITERS OF MERCER ISLAND
Globe Building, Suite 312, 9725 South East 36th Street Mercer Island, WA 98040-3896. Contact James J. Dykeman, Manager. (206) 232-0204. Executive search

THE SEATTLE JOB BANK

firm. Appointment required; no phone calls; unsolicited resumes accepted. Founded 1965. World's largest contingency search firm. Five hundred offices nationwide, doing business under the names "Management Recruiters", "Sales Consultants", "CompuSearch" and "OfficeMates5". Specializes in mid-management/professional positions, $25,000-75,000. Specializes in the areas of: Accounting; Administration, MIS/EDP; Advertising; Affirmative Action; Architecture; Banking and Finance; Communications; Computer Hardware and Software; Construction; Electrical; Engineering; Food Industry; General Management; Health and Medical; Human Resources; Industrial and Interior Design; Insurance; Legal; Manufacturing; Operations Management; Printing and Publishing; Procurement; Real Estate; Retailing; Sales and Marketing; Technical and Scientific; Textiles; Transportation. Contingency.

MANAGEMENT RECRUITERS OF SEATTLE
2510 Fairview Avenue, East Post Office Box 12066, Seattle, WA 98102. Contact Ronda Clark, C.P.C., or Dan Jilka, Co-Managers. (206) 328-0936; FAX (206) 328-3256. Executive search firm. Appointment required; no phone calls; unsolicited resumes accepted. Founded 1965. World's largest contingency search firm. Five hundred offices nationwide, doing business under the names "Management Recruiters", "Sales Consultants", "CompuSearch" and "OfficeMates5". Specializes in mid-management/professional positions, $25,000-75,000. Specializes in the areas of: Accounting; Administration, MIS/EDP; Advertising; Affirmative Action;

Architecture; Banking and Finance; Communications; Computer Hardware and Software; Construction; Electrical; Engineering; Food Industry; General Management; Health and Medical; Human Resources; Industrial and Interior Design; Insurance; Legal; Manufacturing; Operations Management; Printing and Publishing; Procurement; Real Estate; Retailing; Sales and Marketing; Technical and Scientific; Textiles; Transportation. Contingency.

MANAGEMENT RECRUITERS OF TACOMA
The Washington Building, Suite 806, 1019 Pacific Avenue Tacoma, WA 98402-4403. Contact Ron Westover, Manager. (206) 627-1972. Executive search firm. Appointment required; no phone calls; unsolicited resumes accepted. Founded 1965. World's largest contingency search firm. Five hundred offices nationwide, doing business under the names "Management Recruiters", "Sales Consultants", "CompuSearch" and "OfficeMates5". Specializes in mid-management/professional positions, $25,000-75,000. Specializes in the areas of: Accounting; Administration, MIS/EDP; Advertising; Affirmative Action; Architecture; Banking and Finance; Communications; Computer Hardware and Software; Construction; Electrical; Engineering; Food Industry; General Management; Health and Medical; Human Resources; Industrial and Interior Design; Insurance; Legal; Manufacturing; Operations Management; Printing and Publishing; Procurement; Real Estate; Retailing; Sales and Marketing; Technical and Scientific; Textiles; Transportation. Contingency.

MANAGEMENT RECRUITERS OF VANCOUVER

703 Broadway Street, Suite 680, Vancouver, WA 98660-3213. Contact Steve Fox, Manager. (206) 694-2809. Executive search firm. Appointment required; no phone calls; unsolicited resumes accepted. Founded 1965. World's largest contingency search firm. Five hundred offices nationwide, doing business under the names "Management Recruiters", "Sales Consultants", "CompuSearch" and "OfficeMates5". Specializes in mid-management/professional positions, $25,000-75,000. Specializes in the areas of: Accounting; Administration, MIS/EDP; Advertising; Affirmative Action; Architecture; Banking and Finance; Communications; Computer Hardware and Software; Construction; Electrical; Engineering; Food Industry; General Management; Health and Medical; Human Resources; Industrial and Interior Design; Insurance; Legal; Manufacturing; Operations Management; Printing and Publishing; Procurement; Real Estate; Retailing; Sales and Marketing; Technical and Scientific; Textiles; Transportation. Contingency.

OFFICEMATES5 OF SEATTLE

2510 Fairview Avenue, East Post Office Box 12066, Seattle, WA 98102. Contact Ronda Clark, C.P.C., General Manager, or Cheryl Fitzpatrick or Roger Nettleton, Co-Managers. (206) 328-0936; FAX (206) 328-7221. Executive search firm. Appointment required; no phone calls; unsolicited resumes accepted. Founded 1965. World's largest contingency search firm. Five hundred offices nationwide, doing business under the names "Management Recruiters", "Sales Consultants", "CompuSearch" and "OfficeMates5". Specializes in mid-management/professional positions, $25,000-75,000. Specializes in the areas of: Accounting; Administration, MIS/EDP; Advertising; Affirmative Action; Architecture; Banking and Finance; Communications; Computer Hardware and Software; Construction; Electrical; Engineering; Food Industry; General Management; Health and Medical; Human Resources; Industrial and Interior Design; Insurance; Legal; Manufacturing; Operations Management; Printing and Publishing; Procurement; Real Estate; Retailing; Sales and Marketing; Technical and Scientific; Textiles; Transportation. Contingency.

SALES CONSULTANTS OF SEATTLE
Eastridge Corporate Center, Suite 304, 11811 Northeast First Street Bellevue, WA 98005-3094. Contact Paul Komorner, Manager. (206) 455-1805. Executive search firm. Appointment required; no phone calls; unsolicited resumes accepted. Founded 1965. World's largest contingency search firm. Five hundred offices nationwide, doing business under the names "Management Recruiters", "Sales Consultants", "CompuSearch" and "OfficeMates5". Specializes in mid-management/professional positions, $25,000-75,000. Specializes in the areas of: Accounting; Administration, MIS/EDP; Advertising; Affirmative Action; Architecture; Banking and Finance; Communications; Computer Hardware and Software; Construction; Electrical; Engineering; Food Industry; General

Management; Health and Medical; Human Resources; Industrial and Interior Design; Insurance; Legal; Manufacturing; Operations Management; Printing and Publishing; Procurement; Real Estate; Retailing; Sales and Marketing; Technical and Scientific; Textiles; Transportation. Contingency.

Professional Associations

Anyone who has conducted a job search has heard the dictum, "It's not what you know, it's who you know." While the validity of this comment has just as often been exxagerated, it does contain more than a grain of truth. Connections can never replace good old hard work as the best method of finding employment, but they can't hurt.

If you don't have an uncle in high places who can set up some interviews for you with a few of his friends, don't worry. Most people don't. The important thing to remember is that in most instances, connections do not materialize out of thin air -- they are created. That means that anyone who works at it can make them.

One of the best ways to meet people in your area of interest is through professional trade associations. Trade associations exist so that professionals in an industry can meet, share information about trends in the field, and arrange new business. Many of them regularly publish newsletters and magazines that will help you stay abreast of the current state of your industry. In addition, many associations hold regular meetings, and these meetings may present you the opportunity not only to learn more about the field you hope to enter, but also to establish connections.

With this in mind, we have included this directory of professional associations. Many of the addresses listed are for headquarters offices only. Inquire about local chapters in your area.

Air Line Employees Association
5600 South Central Ave
Chicago IL 60638
312/767-3333

Air Transport Association of America
1709 New York Ave NW
Washington DC 20006
202/626-4000

American Academy of Actuaries
1720 I Street NW, Suite 700
Washington DC 20006
202/223-8196

American Academy of Family Physicians
8880 Ward Parkway
Kansas City, MO 64114
816/333-9700

American Association. of
Advertising Agencies
666 Third Avenue
New York NY 10017
212/682-2500

American Association of Cereal Chemists
3340 Pilot Knob Road
St. Paul, MN 55121
612/454-7250

**American Association of
Zoological Parks & Aquariums**
Oglebay Park,
Wheeling, WV 26003
304/242-2160

**American Association for
Clinical Chemistry**
2029 K Street NW, 7th Floor
Washington., DC 20006
202/857-0717

**American Association of
Petroleum Geologists**
1444 South Boulder,
Tulsa, OK 74119
918/584-2555

**American Association of
School Administrators**
1801 North Moore Street
Arlington, VA 22209
703/528-0700

American Bankers Association
1120 Connecticut Avenue NW
Washington DC 20036
202/663-5221

American Bar Association
750 North Lake Shore Drive
Chicago, IL 60611
312/988-5000

American Booksellers Association
137 West 25th Street
New York, NY 10001
212/463-8450

American Chemical Society
1155 16th Street NW
Washington, DC 20036
202/872-4600

American Council of Life Insurance
1001 Pennsylvania Avenue NW,
Washington, DC 20004
202/624-2000

American Dental Association
211 East Chicago Avenue
Chicago, IL 60611
312/440-2500

**American Electroplaters
and Surface Finishers Society**
12644 Research Parkway,
Orlando, FL 32826
407/281-6441

American Federation of Small Business
407 South Dearborn Street
Chicago, IL 60605
312/427-0206

**American Federation of Television
and Radio Artists**
260 Madison Avenue
New York, NY 10016
212/532-0800

American Gas Association
1515 Wilson Boulevard,
Arlington, VA 22209
703/841-8400

American Geological Institute
4220 King Street
Alexandria, VA 22302
703/379-2480

**American Institute of Aeronautics
and Astronautics**
555 West 57th Street
New York, NY 10019
212/247-6500

American Institute of Architects
1735 New York Ave NW
Washington DC 20006
202/626-7300

**American Institute of
Certified Public Accountants**
1211 Avenue of the Americas
New York NY 10036
212/575-6200

American Institute of Chemical Engineers
345 East 47th Street
New York, NY 10017
212/705-7338

American Institute of Chemists
7315 Wisconsin Avenue
Bethesda, MD 20814
301/652-2447

American Institute of Mining, Metallurgical and Petroleum
345 East 47th Street
New York, NY 10017
212/705-7695

American Insurance Association
1130 Connecticut Avenue NW,
Suite 1000
Washington, DC 20036
202/828-7100

American Caste Metals Association
455 State Street
Des Plaines, IL 60016
312/299-9156

American Marketing Association
250 South Wacker Drive,
Suite 200
Chicago, IL 60606
312/648-0536

American Medical Association
535 North Dearborn Street
Chicago, IL 60610
312/645-5000

**American Newspaper
Publishers Association**
11600 Sunrise Valley Drive
Reston, VA 22091
703/648-1000

American Nuclear Society
555 North Kensington Avenue
La Grange Park, IL 60525
312/352-6611

American Paper Institute
260 Madison Avenue
New York, NY 10016
212/340-0600

American Petroleum Institute
1220 L Street NW,
Washington, DC 20005
202/682-8000

American Pharmaceutical Association
2215 Constitution Avenue NW,
Washington, DC 20037
202/628-4410

American Physical Therapy Association
1111 North Fairfax Street

Alexandria, VA 22314
703/684-2782

American Powder Metallurgy Institute
105 College Road East,
Princeton, NJ 08540
609/452-7700

**American Society for Biochemistry
and Molecular Biology**
9650 Rockville Pike,
Bethesda, MD 20814
301/530-7145

**American Society for
Engineering Education**
11 Dupont Circle NW,
Suite 200,
Washington, DC 20036
202/293-7080

**American Society of
Agricultural Engineers**
2950 Niles Road
St. Joseph, MI 49085
616/429-0300

American Society of Appraisers
P.O. Box 17265
Washington DC 20041
202/478-2228

American Society of Brewing Chemists
3340 Pilot Knob Road
St. Paul, MN 55121
612/454-7250

American Society of Civil Engineers
345 East 47th Street
New York, NY 10017
212/705-7496

American Society of Heating, Refrigerating & Air Conditioning Engineers
1791 Tullie Circle NE,
Atlanta, GA 30329
404/636-8400

American Society of Landscape Architects
1733 Connecticut Avenue NW,
Washington, DC 20009
202/466-7730

American Society of Naval Engineers
1452 Duke Street
Alexandria, VA 22314
703/836-6727

American Society of Newspaper Editors
P.O. Box 17004,
Washington, DC 20041
202/620-6087

American Society of Plumbing Engineers
3617 Thousand Oaks Boulevard,

Suite #210
Westlake Village, CA 91362-3625
805/495-7120

American Society of Safety Engineers
1800 East Oakton Street,
Des Plaines, IL 60018
312/692-4121

American Society of Tribologists and Lubrication Engineers
838 Busse Highway,
Park Ridge, IL 60068
312/825-5536

American Textile Manufacturers Institute
1801 K Street NW,
Suite 900,
Washington, DC 20006
202/862-0500

American Society of Travel Agents
1101 King Street,
Alexandria, VA 22314
703/739-2782

American Trucking Association
2200 Mill Road
Alexandria, VA 22314
703/838-1700

American Veterinary Medical Association
930 North Meacham Road

Schaumburg, IL 60196
312/605-8070

American Water Works Association
6666 West Quincy Avenue
Denver, CO 80235
303/794-7711

Association of American Publishers
220 East 23rd Street
New York, NY 10010
212/689-8920

Association of American Universities
One Dupont Circle NW,
Suite 730
Washington, DC 20036
202/466-5030

Association for Computing Machinery
11 West 42nd Street
New York, NY 10036
212/869-7440

Association of American Railroads
50 F Street NW
Washington DC 20001
202/639-2100

Association of Iron and Steel Engineers
Three Gateway Center,
Suite 2350

Pittsburgh, PA 15222
412/281-6323

Association of Legal Administrators
104 Wilmot,
Suite 205,
Deerfield, IL 60015-5195
312/940-9240

Association of State & Interstate Water Pollution Control Administrators
444 North Capital Street NW,
Suite #330,
Washington, DC 20001
202/624-7782

Business-Professional Advertising Association
Metroplex Corporate Center
100 Metroplex Drive
Edison, NJ 08817
201/985-4441

Clean Energy Research Institute
P.O. Box 248294,
Coral Gables, FL 33124
305/284-4666

Construction Industry Manufacturers Association
111 East Wisconsin Avenue
Milwaukee, WI 53202
414/272-0943

**Dairy and Food Industries
Supply Association**
6245 Executive Boulevard
Rockville, MD 20852
301/984-1444

**Drug, Chemical and Allied
Trades Association**
#2 Two Roosevelt Avenue
3rd Floor
Syosset, NY 11791
516/496-3317

Electrochemical Society
10 South Main Street
Pennington, NJ 08534
609/737-1902

Electronic Industries Association
1722 Eye Street NW,
Suite 300
Washington, DC 20006
202/457-4900

Federal Bar Association,
1815 H Street NW
Washington, DC 20006
202/638-0252

Federation of Tax Administrators
444 North Capital Street NW,

Washington, DC 20001
202/624-5890

Financial Analysts Federation
1633 Broadway,
Room 1602
New York, NY 10019
212/957-2860

Financial Executives Institute
10 Madison Avenue,
P.O. Box 1938,
Morristown, NJ 07960
201/898-4600

Geological Society of America
3300 Penrose Place,
P.O. Box 9140,
Boulder, CO 80301
303/447-2020

Illuminating Engineering Society of North America
345 East 47th Street
New York, NY 10017
212/705-7926

Independent Bankers Association. of America
One Thomas Circle NW,
Suite 950
Washington DC 20005
202/659-8111

**Institute of Electrical and
Electronics Engineers**
345 East 47th Street
New York, NY 10017
212/705-7900

Institute of Industrial Engineers
25 Technology Park,
Atlanta, GA 30092
404/449-0460

Institute of Management Consultants
19 West 44th Street
New York, NY 10036
212/921-2885

Institute of Transportation Engineers
Suite 410,
525 School Street NW,
Washington, DC 20024
202/554-8050

**International Circulation
Managers Association**
11600 Sunrise Valley Drive
Reston, VA 22091
703/620-9555

International Radio and TV Society
420 Lexington Avenue,
Suite 531

New York, NY 10170
212/867-6650

International Real Estate Institute
8383 East Evans Road
Scottsdale, AZ 85260
602/998-8267

Internationl Society of Certified Electronics Technicians
2708 West Berry,
Ft. Worth, TX 76109
817/921-9101

Magazine Publishers Association
575 Lexington Avenue
New York, NY 10022
212/752-0055

Marine Technology Society
1825 K Street NW,
Suite 203
Washington, DC 20009
202/775-5966

Motor Vehicle Manufacturers Association
7430 2nd Avenue,
Suite 300
Detroit, MI 48202
313/872-4311

National Academy of Engineering
2101 Constitution Avenue NW,

Washington, DC 20418
202/334-3200

National Aeronautic Associationn. of USA
1763 R Street NW
Washington DC 20005
202/265-8720

National Agricultural Chemicals Association
1155 15th Street NW,
Suite 900
Washington DC 20005
202/296-1585

National Association. of Accountants
10 Paragon Drive
Box 433
Montvale NJ 07645
201/573-9000

National Association of Business and Educational Radio
1501 Duke Street
Suite 200
Alexandria, VA 22314
703/739-0300

National Association of Credit Management
8815 Centre Park Drive,
Suite 200

Columbia, MD 21045-2117
301/740-5560

National Association of Home Builders
15th & M Streets NW
Washington, DC 20005
202/822-0200

National Association of Manufacturers
1331 Pennsylvania Avenue, NW
Suite 1500
Washington, DC 20004-1703
202/637-3000

National Association of Metal Finishers
111 East Wacker Drive
Chicago, IL 60601
312/644-6610

National Association of Real Estate Investment Trusts
1129 20th Street NW,
Suite 705
Washington DC 20036
202/785-8717

National Association of Social Workers
7981 Eastern Avenue
Silver Spring, MD 20910
301/565-0333

National Automobile Dealers Association
8400 Westpark Drive

Mclean VA 22102
703/821-7000

**National Cooperative
Business Association**
1401 New York Ave. NW,
Suite #1100,
Washington, DC 20005
202/638-6222

National Council of Savings Institutions
1101 15th Street NW,
Suite 400
Washington DC 20005
202/857-3100

National Dairy Council
6300 North River Road
Rosemont, IL 60018
312/696-1020

**National Electrical
Manufacturers Association**
2101 L Street NW
Washington, DC 20037
202/457-8400

**National Electronics
Sales and Services Association**
2708 West Berry,
Ft. Worth, TX 76109
817/921-9061

National Health Council
622 Third Avenue
34th Floor,
New York, NY 10017
212/972-2700

**National Marine
Manufacturers Association**
401 North Michigan Avenue,
Suite 1150
Chicago, IL 60611
312/836-4747

National Medical Association
1012 Tenth Street NW,
Washington, DC 20001
202/347-1895

National Press Club
529 14th St. NW
Washington DC 20045
202/662-7500

National Small Business United
1155 15th Street NW,
Suite 710
Washington DC 20005
202/293-8830

**National Society of
Professional Engineers**
1420 King Street,

Alexandria, VA 22314
703/684-2800

National Society of Public Accountants
1010 North Fairfax
Alexandria VA 22314
703/549-6400

Northern Textile Association
230 Congress Street
Boston, MA 02110
617/542-8220

Petroleum Equipment Institute
3739 East 31st Street,
P.O. Box 2380/74101
Tulsa, OK 74135
918/743-9941

Printing Industries of America
1730 North Lynn Street
Arlington, VA 22209
703/841-8100

Public Relations Society of America
33 Irving Place
New York,NY 10003
212/995-2230

Shipbuilders Council of America
1110 Vermont Ave. NW
Washington DC 20005
202/775-9060

Society of Actuaries
475 North Martingale Road,
Suite 800
Schaumburg, IL 60173
312/706-3500

Society of Exploration Geophysicists
P.O. Box 702740,
8801 South Yale,
Tulsa, OK 74170-2740
918/493-3516

Society of Fire Protection Engineers
60 Batterymarch Street
Boston, MA 02110
617/482-0686

Society of Plastics Industry
355 Lexington Avenue
New York, NY 10017
212/370-7340

Society of Plastic Engineers
14 Fairfield Drive,
Brookfield Centre, CT 06804
203/775-0471

**Technical Association of
the Pulp and Paper Industry**
P.O. Box 105113,
Atlanta, GA 30348
404/446-1400

Television Bureau of Advertising
477 Madison Avnenue
New York, NY 10022-5892
212/486-1111

United Engineering Trustees
345 East 47th Street
New York, NY 10017
212/705-7000

Water Pollution Control Federation
601 Wythe Street Avenue NW,
Alexandria, VA 22314
703/684-2400

West Writers Guild of America
8955 Beverly Boulevard,
Los Angeles, CA 90048
213/550-1000

Women in Radio and TV, Inc.
1101 Connecticut Avenue NW,
Suite 700
Washington, DC 20036
202/429-5102

The Basics of Job Winning

The Basics of Job Winning
A Condensed Review

The best way to obtain a better professional job is to contact the employer directly. Broad-based statistical studies by the Department of Labor show that job seekers have found employment more successfully by contacting employers directly, than by using any other method.

However, given the current diversity, and increased specialization of both industry and job tasks it is possible that in some situations other job seeking methods may prove at least equally successful. Three of the other most commonly used methods are: relying on personal contacts, using employment services, and following up help wanted advertisements. Many professionals have been successful in finding better jobs using one of these methods. However, the Direct Contact method has an overall success rate twice that of any other method and it has been successfully used by many more professionals. So unless you have specific reasons to believe that another method would work best for you, the Direct Contact method should form the foundation of your job search effort.

The Objective

With any business task, you must develop a strategy for meeting a goal. This is especially true when it comes to obtaining a better job. First you need to clearly define your objectives.

Setting your job objectives is better known as career planning (or life planning for those who wish to emphasize the importance of combining the two). Career planning has become a field of study in and of itself. Since most of our readers are probably well-entrenched in their career path, we will touch on career planning just briefly.

If you are thinking of choosing or switching careers, we particularly emphasize two things. First choose a career where you will enjoy most of the day-to-day tasks. Sure, this sounds obvious, but most of us have at one point or another been attracted by a glamour industry or a prestigious sounding job without thinking of the most important consideration: Would we enjoy performing the everyday tasks the position entailed?

The second key consideration is that you are not merely choosing a career, but also a lifestyle. Career counselors indicate that one of the most common problems people encounter in job seeking is a lack of consideration for how well-suited they are for a particular position or career. For example, some people, attracted to management consulting by good salaries, early responsibility and high level corporate exposure, do not adapt well to the long hours, heavy travel demands, and the constant pressure to produce. So be sure to determine both for your career as a whole and for each position that you apply for, if you will easily adapt to both the day-to-day duties that the position entails and the working environment.

The Strategy

Assuming that you have now established your career objectives, the next step of the job search is to develop a strategy. If you don't take the time to develop a strategy and lay out a plan you will probably find yourself going in circles after several weeks making a random search for opportunities that always seem just beyond your reach.

Your strategy can be thought as having three simple elements:

1. Choose a method of contacting employers.

2. Allocating your scarce resources (in most job searches the key scarce resource will be time, but financial considerations will become important in some searches too).

3. Evaluating how the selected contact method is working and then considering adopting other methods.

We suggest you give serious consideration to using the Direct Contact method exclusively. However, we realize it is human nature to avoid putting all your eggs in one basket. So, if you prefer to use other methods as well, try to expend at least half your effort on the Direct Contact method, spending the rest on all of the other

Developing Your Contacts (Networking)

Some career counselors feel that the best route to a better job is through somebody you already know or through somebody to whom you can be introduced. The counselors recommend you build your contact base beyond your current acquaintances by asking them to each introduce you, or refer you, to additional people in your field of interest.

The theory goes like this: You might start with 15 personal contacts, each of whom introduces you to 3 additional people, for a total of 45 additional contacts. Then each of these people introduces you to 3 additional people which adds 135 additional contacts. Who in turn introduce you to 405 additional contacts. Theoretically you will soon know every person in the entire industry.

Of course, developing your personal contacts does not usually work quite as smoothly as the theory suggests because some people will not be able to introduce you to several relevant additional contacts. The further you stray from your initial contact base, the weaker your references will be. So, if you do try developing your own contacts, try to begin with as large an initial group of people you personally know as possible. Dig into your personal phone book and your holiday greeting card list and locate old classmates from school. Be particularly sure to approach people who perform your personal business such as your lawyer, accountant, banker, doctor, stockbroker and insurance agent. These people develop a very broad contact base due to the nature of their professions.

methods combined. Millions of other job seekers have already proven that Direct Contact has been twice as effective in obtaining employment, so why not benefit from their effort?

With your strategy in mind, the next step is to develop the details of the plan, or scheduling. Of course, job searches are not something that most people do regularly so it is difficult to estimate how long each step will take. Nonetheless, it is important to have a plan so that your effort can be allocated the way you have chosen, so that you can see yourself progressing, and to facilitate reconsideration of your chosen strategy.

It is important to have a realistic time frame in mind. If you will be job searching full-time, your search will probably take at least two months and very likely, substantially longer. If you can only devote part-time effort, it will probably take four months.

You probably know a few people who seem to spend their whole lives searching for a better job in their part time. Don't be one of them. Once you begin your job search, on a part-time basis, give it your whole-hearted effort. If you don't really feel like devoting a lot of energy to job seeking right now, then wait. Focus on enjoying your present position, performing your best on the job, and storing up energy for when you are really ready to begin your job search.

Those of you currently unemployed, should remember that job hunting is tough work physically and emotionally. It is also intellectually demanding - requiring your best. So don't tire yourself out by working on your job campaign around the clock. It would be counter-productive. At the same time be sure to discipline yourself. The most logical approach to time management is to keep your regular working hours.

For those of you who are still employed, job searching will be particularly tiring because it must be done in addition to your regular duties. So don't work yourself to the point where you show up to interviews appearing exhausted and slip behind at your current job. But don't be tempted to quit! The long hours are worth it - it is much easier to sell your skills from a position of strength (as someone currently employed).

If you are searching full-time and have decided to choose a mixture of contact methods, we recommend that you divide up each week allowing some time for each method. For instance, you might devote Mondays to following-up newspaper ads because most of them appear in Sunday papers. Then you might devote Tuesdays, and Wednesday mornings to working and developing the personal contacts you have, in addition to trying a few employment services. Then you could devote the rest of the week to the Direct Contact method. This is just one plan that may succeed for you.

By trying several methods at once, job-searching will be more interesting for you, and you will be able to evaluate how promising each of the methods seems, altering your time allocation accordingly. Be very careful in your evaluation, however, and don't judge the success of a particular method just by the sheer number of interviews you obtain. Positions advertised in the newspaper, for instance, are likely to generate many more interviews per opening than positions that are filled without being advertised.

If you are searching part-time and decide to try several different contact methods, we recommend that you try them sequentially. You simply won't have enough time to put a meaningful amount of effort into more than one method at once. So decide how long your job search might take. (Only a guess, of course.) And then allocate so many weeks or months for each contact method you choose to use. (We suggest that you try Direct Contact first).

If you are expected to be in your office during the business day then you have an additional time problem to deal with. How can you work interviews into the business day? And if you work in an open office, how can you even call to set up interviews? As much as possible you should keep up the effort and the appearances on your present job. So maximize your use of the lunch hour, early in the morning and late in the afternoon for calling. If you really keep trying you will be surprised how often you will be able to reach the executive you are trying to contact during your out-of-office hours. The lunch hour for different executives will vary between 12 and 3. Also you can catch people as early as 8 AM and as late as 6 PM on frequent occasions. Jot out a plan each night on how you will be using each minute of your precious lunch break.

Your inability to interview at any time other than lunch just might work to your advantage. If you can, try to set up as many interviews as possible for your lunch hour. This will go a long way to creating a relaxed rapport. (Who isn't happy when eating?) But be sure the interviews don't stray too far from the agenda on hand.

Lunchtime inteviews will be much easier for the person with substantial career experience to obtain. People with less experience will often find that they have no alternative other than taking time off for interviewing. If you have to take time off, you have to take time off. But try to do this as little as possible. Usually you should take the whole day off so that it is not blatantly obvious that you are job searching. Try to schedule in at least two, or at the most three, interviews for the same day. (It is very difficult to maintain an optimum level of energy at more than three interviews in one day.) Explain to the interviewer why you might have to juggle your interview schedule - he/she should honor the respect you are showing your current employer by minimizing your days off and will probably appreciate the fact that another prospective employer is showing an interest in you.

Once again we need to emphasize if you are searching for a job, especially part-time, get out there and do the necessary tasks to the best of your ability and get it over with. Don't let your job search drag on endlessly.

Remember that all schedules are meant to be broken. The purpose of a schedule in your job search is not to rush you to your goal, its purpose is to map out the road ahead of you and to evaluate the progress of your chosen strategy to date.

Don't Bother To Try Mass Mail or Phone Call Barrages

Direct Contact does not mean burying every firm within a one-hundred mile radius with mail and phone calls. Mass-mail techniques very very seldom work. This applies equally to those letters that are personalized (but dehumanized) on an automatic typewriter. Don't waste your time or money on such a project; you will fool no one but yourself. The same applies for making a barrage of phone calls.

The worst part of sending out a mass mailing or making unplanned phone calls is that you are likely to be remembered only as someone with little genuine interest in the firm, as someone who lacks sincerity, and as someone that nobody wants to hire.

Help-Wanted Advertisements

Only a small fraction of professional job openings are advertised. Yet a majority of job seekers (and a lot of people not in the job market) spend much time studying the help-wanted ads. As a result the competition for advertised openings is often severe.

A moderate-sized Manhattan employer told us this about an experience advertising in the help-wanted section of a major Sunday newspaper:

> It was a disaster. We had over 500 responses from this relatively small ad in just one week. We have only two phone lines in this office and one was totally knocked out. We will never do it (advertise for professional help) again.

If you still insist on following-up the help-wanted ads, then research a firm before you reply to the ad so that you can ascertain the fact that you would really be a suitable candidate and that you would enjoy working at a particular firm. Also such preliminary research might help to separate you from all of the other professionals responding to the ad, many of whom will only have a passing interest in the opportunity. However, as your odds of obtaining a better job through the want ads are still small, do not invest a lot of effort in this job-seeking method.

The Direct Contact Method

Once you have scheduled a time you are ready to begin using the job search method that you have chosen. In the text we will restrict discussion to use of the Direct Contact method. Sideboards will comment briefly on developing your personal contacts and using newspaper advertisements.

The first step in preparing for Direct Contact is to develop a check list for categorizing the types of firms for which you would prefer working. You might categorize firms by their product line, their size, their customer-type (such as industrial or consumer), their growth prospects, or, of course, by their geographical locations. Your list of important considerations might be very short. If if is, good! The shorter it is, the easier it will be to find appropriate firms.

Then try to decide at which firms you are most likely to be able to obtain employment. You might wish to consider to what degree your particular skills might be in demand, the degree of competition for employment, and the employment outlook at the firm.

Now you are ready to assemble your list of prospective employers. Build up your list to at least 100 prospects. Then separate your prospect list into three groups. The first tier of maybe 25 firms will be your primary target market, the second group of another 25 firms will be your secondary market, and the remaining names you will keep in reserve.

This book will help you greatly in developing your prospect list. Turn to the industry cross index to get started. Then refer back to the alphabetically ordered employer listings to obtain more information about each firm.

At this stage, once you have gotten your prospect list together and have an idea of the firms for which you might wish to work, it is best to get to work on your resume. Refer to formats of the sample resumes included in this section of the book.

Once your resume is at the printer, begin research for the first batch of 25 prospective employers. You will want to determine whether you would be happy working at the firmsyou are researching and also get a better idea of what their employment needs might be. You also need to obtain enough information to sound highly informed about the company during phone conversations and in mail correspondence. But don't go all out on your research yet! At some of these firms you probably will not be able to arrange interviews, so save your big research effort until you start to arrange interviews. Nevertheless, you should plan to spend about 3 or 4 hours, on average, researching each firm. Do your research in batches to save time and energy. Go into one resource at a time and find out what you can about each of the 25 firms in the batch. Start with the easiest resources to use (such as this book). Keep organized. Maintain a folder on each firm.

If you discover something that really disturbs you about the firm (i.e. perhaps they are about to close their only local office) or if you discover that your chances of getting a job there are practically nil (i.e. perhaps they just instituted a hiring freeze) then cross them off your prospect list.

If possible, supplement your research efforts with contacts to individuals who know the firm well. Ideally you should make an informal contact with someone at the particular firm, but often a contact at a direct competitor, or a major supplier or customer will be able to supply you with just as much information. At the very least try to obtain whatever printed information that the company has available, not just annual reports, but product brochures and anything else. The company might very well have printed information about career opportunities.

Getting The Interview

Now it is time to arrange an interview, time to make the Direct Contact. If you have read many books on job searching you have probably noticed that virtually all tell you to avoid the personnel office like the plague. It is said that the personnel office never hires people, they just screen out candidates. In some cases you may be able to identify and contact the appropriate manager with the authority to hire you. However, this will take a lot of time and effort in each case. Often you'll be bounced back to personnel. So we suggest that you begin your Direct Contact campaign through personnel offices. If it seems that in the firms on your prospect list that little hiring is done through personnel, you might consider an alternative course of action.

The three obvious means of initiating Direct Contact are:

-Showing up unannounced
-Phone calls
-Mail

Cross out the first one right away. You should never show up to seek a professional position without an appointment. Even if you are somehow lucky enough to obtain an interview, you will appear so unprofessional that you will not even be seriously considered.

Mail contact seems to be a good choice if you have not been in the job market for a while. You can take your time to prepare a careful letter, say exactly what you want, tuck your resume in, and then the addressee can read the material at leisure. But employers receive many resumes every day. Don't be surprised if you do not get a response to your inquiry. So don't spend weeks waiting for responses that never come. If you do send a cover letter, follow-up (or precede it) with a phone call. This will increase your impact, and underscore both your interest in the firm and the fact that you are familiar with it (because of the initial research you did).

Another alternative is to make a "Cover Call." Your Cover Call should be just like your cover letter: concise. Your first sentence should interest the employer in you. Then try to subtly mention your familiarity with the firm. Don't be overbearing; keep your introduction to three sentences or less. Be pleasant, self confident and relaxed. This will greatly increase the chances of the person at the other end of the line developing the conversation. But don't press. When you are asked to follow up "with something in the mail" don't try to prolong the conversation once it has ended. Don't ask what they want to receive in the mail. Always send your resume and a highly personalized follow-up letter, reminding the addressee of the phone conversation.

Some Favorite Interview Questions

Tell me about yourself...
Why did you leave your last job?
What excites you in your current job?
What are your career goals?
Where would you like to be in 5 years?
What are your greatest strengths?
What are your greatest weaknesses?
Why do you wish to work for this firm?
Where else are you seeking employment?
Why should we hire you?

Always include a cover letter even if you are requested to send a resume. (It is assumed that you will send a cover letter too).

Unless you are in telephone sales, making smooth and relaxed Cover Calls will probably not come easily. Practice them on your own and then with your friends or relatives (friends are likely to be more objective and hence, better participants).

If you obtain an interview over the telephone, be sure to send a thank you note reiterating the points you made during the conversation. You will appear more professional and increase your impact. However, don't mail your resume once an interview has been arranged unless it is specifically requested. Take it with you to the interview instead.

Preparing For The Interview

Once the interview has been arranged, begin your in-depth research. You have got to arrive at the interview knowing the company upside down and inside out. You need to know their products, their types of customers, their subsidiaries, their parent, their principle locations, their rank in the industry, their sales and profit trends, their type of ownership, their size, their current plans and much more. By this time you have probably narrowed your job search to one industry, but if you haven't then you need to be familiar with the trends in this firm's industry, the firm's principle competitors and their relative performance, and the direction that the industry leaders are headed. Dig into every resource you can! All the company literature, the trade press, the business press, and if they are public call your stockbroker and ask for still additional information. If possible, speak to someone at the firm before the interview, or if not, speak to someone at a competing firm. Clearly the more time you spend, the better. Even if you feel extremely pressed for time, you should set aside at least 12 hours for pre-interview research.

If you have been out of the job market for some time, don't be surprised if you find yourself tense during your first few interviews. It will probably happen every time you re-enter the market, not just when you seek your first job after getting out of school.

Tension is natural during an interview, but if you can be relaxed you will have an advantage over the competition. Knowing you have done a thorough research job should help you relax for an interview. Also make a list of the questions that you think might be asked in an interview. Think out your answers carefully. Then practice reviewing them with a friend. Tape record your responses to the questions he/she raises in the role as interviewer. If you feel particularly unsure of your interviewing skills, arrange your first interviews at firms in which you are not very interested. (But remember it is common courtesy to seem excited about the possibility of working for any firm at which you interview.) Then practice again on your own after these first few interviews. Go over each of the questions that you were asked.

How important is the proper dress for a job interview? Buying a complete wardrobe of Brooks Brothers pinstripes, donning new wing tip shoes and having your hair trimmed every morning is not enough to guarantee your obtaining a career position as an investment banker. But on the other hand, if you can't find a clean, conservative suit and a narrow tie, or won't take the time to polish your shoes and trim and wash your hair--then you are just wasting your time by interviewing at all.

Very rarely will the final selection of candidates for a job opening be determined by dress. So don't spend a fortune on a new wardrobe. But be sure that your clothes are adequate.

Men applying for any professional position should wear a suit; women should either wear a dress or a suit (not a pant suit). Your clothes should be at least as formal or slightly more formal than those worn by the people on the level of position for which you are applying. When in doubt it is better to be slightly more formal and more conservative than the position would suggest.

Top personal grooming is more important than finding the perfect clothes for a job interview. Careful grooming indicates both a sense of thoroughness and self-confidence.

Be sure that your clothes fit well and that they are immaculately clean. Hair must be neatly trimmed and freshly washed. Shoes should be newly polished. Women need to avoid excessive jewelry and excessive make-up. Men ought to appear freshly shaven, even if the interview is late in the day.

Be complete. Everyone needs a watch and a pen and pad of paper (for taking notes). Finally a briefcase or folder (containing extra copies of your resume) will help complete the look of professionalism.

Sometimes the interviewer will be running behind schedule. Don't be upset, be sympathetic. He might be under pressure to interview a lot of candidates and to quickly fill a demanding position. So be sure to come to your interview with good reading material to keep yourself occupied. This will help increase your patience and ease your tenseness.

The Interview

The very beginning of the interview is the most important part because it determines the rapport for the rest of it. Those first few moments are especially crucial. Do you smile when you meet? Do you establish enough eye contact, but not too much? Do you walk into the office with a self-asssured and confident stride? Do you shake hands firmly? Do you make small talk easily without being garrulous? It is human nature to judge people by that first impression, so make sure it is a good one. But most of all, try to be yourself.

Often the interviewer will begin, after the small talk, by proceeding to tell you about the company, the division, the department, or perhaps, the position. Because of your detailed research, the information about the company will be repetitive for you and the interviewer would probably like nothing better than to avoid this regurgitation of the company biography. So if you can do so tactfully, indicate to the interviewer that you are very familiar with the firm. If he/she seems intent on providing you with background information, despite your hints, then acquiesce. But be sure to remain attentive. If you can manage to generate a brief discussion of the company or the industry at this point, without being forceful, great. It will help to further build rapport, underscore your interests and increase your impact.

Soon (if it didn't begin that way) the interviewer will begin the questions. This period of the interview falls into one of two categories (or somewhere in between): either a structured interview, where the interviewer has a prescribed set of questions to ask; or an unstructured interview, where the interviewer will ask only leading questions to get you to talk about yourself, your experiences and your goals. Try to sense as quickly as possible which direction the interview wishes to proceed and follow along in the direction he/she seems to be leading. This will make the interviewer feel more relaxed and in control of the situation.

Many of the questions will be similiar to the ones that you were expecting and you will have prepared answers. Remember to keep attuned to the interviewer and make the length of your answers appropriate to the situation. If you are really unsure as to how detailed a response the interviewer is seeking, then ask. Query if he/she would prefer more details of a particular aspect.

As the interview progresses, the interviewer will probably mention what he/she considers to be the most important responsibilities of the position. If applicable, draw parallels between your experience and the demands of the position as seen by the interviewer. Describe your past experience in the same manner that you did on your resume: emphasizing results and achievements and not merely describing activities. If you listen carefully (listening is a very important part of the interviewing process) the interviewer might very well mention or imply the skills in terms of what the interviewer is seeking. But don't exaggerate. Be on the level.

Try not to cover too much ground during the first interview. This interview is often the toughest, with many candidates being screened out. If you are interviewing for a very competitive position, you will have to make an impression that will last. Focus on a few of your greatest strengths that are relevant to the position. Develop these points carefully, state them again in other words, and then try to summarize them briefly at the end of the interview.

Often the interviewer will pause towards the end and ask if you have any questions? Particularly in a structured interview, this might be the one chance to really show your knowledge of and interest in the firm. Have prepared a list of specific questions that are of real interest to you. Let your questions subtly show your research and your extensive knowledge of the firm's activities. It is wise to have an extensive list of questions, as several of them may have already been answered during the interview.

Do not allow your opportunity to ask questions become an interrogation. Avoid bringing your list of questions to the interview. And ask questions that you are fairly certain the interviewer can answer (remember how you feel when you cannot answer a question during an interview).

Even if you are unable to determine the salary range beforehand, do not ask about it during the first interview. You can always ask about it later. Above all, don't ask about fringe benefits until you have been offered a position. (Then be sure to get all the details.)

You're Fired!!

- You are not the first and you will not be last to go through this traumatic experience. Thousands of professionals are fired every week.
- Being fired is not a reflection on you as a person. It is usually a reflection of your company's staffing needs and its perception of your recent job performance.
- Share the fact with your relatives and friends. Being fired is not something of which to be ashamed.
- Don't start your job search with a flurry of unplanned activity. Start by choosing a strategy and working out a plan.
- Now is not the time for major changes in your life. If possible, remain in the same career and in the same geographical location, at least until you have been working again for a while. On the other hand, if the only industry for which you are trained is leaving, or is severely depressed in your area, then you should give prompt consideration to moving or switching careers.
- Register for unemployment compensation immediately. A thorough job search could take months. After all, your employers have been contributing to unemployment insurance specifically for you ever since your first job. Don't be surprised to find other professionals collecting unemployment compensation also. Unemployment compensation is for everybody who is between jobs.
- Be prepared to answer the question during job interviews of why you think you were fired. Avoid mentioning you were fired while arranging interviews. Try especially hard not to speak negatively of your past employer and not to sound particularly worried about your current, temporarily-unemployed status.
- Do not spend much time reflecting on why you were fired or how you might have avoided it. Look ahead. Think positively. And be sure to follow a careful plan during your job search.

You should be able to determine the company's policy on fringe benefits relatively easily before the interview.

Try not to be negative about anything during the interview. (Particularly any past employer or any previous job.) Be cheerful. Everyone likes to work with someone who seems to be happy.

Don't let a tough question throw you off base. If you don't know the answer to a question, say so simply-do not apologize. Just smile. Nobody can answer every question--particularly some of the questions that are asked in job interviews.

Before your first interview, you may have been able to determine how many interviews the employer usually has for positions at your level. (Of course it may differ quite a bit within one firm.) Usually you can count on at least three or four interviews, although some firms, such as some of the professional partnerships, are well-known to give a minimum of six interviews for all professional positions.

Depending on what information you are able to obtain you might want to vary your strategy quite a bit from interview to interview. For instance if the first interview is a screening interview then try to have a few of your strengths really stand out. On the other hand, if later interviews are primarily with people who are in a position to veto your hiring, but not to push it forward (and few people are weeded out at these stages), then you should primarily focus on building rapport as opposed to reiterating and developing your key strengths.

If it looks as though your skills and background do not match the position your interviewer was hoping to fill, ask him or her if there is another division or subsidiary that perhaps could profit from your talents.

After The Interview

Write a follow-up letter immediately after the interview, while the interview is still fresh in the interviewer's mind. Then, if you have not heard from the interviewer within seven days, call him/her to stress your continued interest in the firm and the position and to request a second interview.

A parting word of advice. Again and again during your job search you will be rejected. You will be rejected when you apply for interviews. You will be rejected after interviews. For every job you finally receive you will probably have received a multitude of rejections. Don't let these rejections slow you down. Keep reminding yourself that the sooner you go out and get started on your job search and get those rejections flowing in, the closer you will be to obtaining the better job.

Resumes and Cover Letters

THE SEATTLE JOB BANK

This Section Contains:

1. Resume Preparation

2. Resume Format

3. Resume Content

4. Should You Hire A Resume Writer?

5. Sample Resumes

6. Cover Letter Preparation

7. General Model for a Cover Letter

8. Sample Cover Letters

9. General Model for a Follow-up Letter

RESUMES/OVERVIEW

When filling a position, a recruiter will often have 100 plus applicants, but time to interview only the

5 or 10 most promising ones. So he will have to reject most applicants after a brief skimming of their resume.

Unless you have phoned and talked to the recruiter-which you should do whenever you can-you will be chosen or rejected for an interview entirely on the basis of your resume and cover letter. So your resume must be outstanding. (But remember-a resume is not a substitution for a job search campaign. YOU must seek a job. Your resume is only one tool.)

RESUME PREPARATION

One page, usually.

Unless you have an unusually strong background with many years of experience and a large diversity of outstanding achievements, prepare a one page resume. Recruiters dislike long resumes.

8 1/2 x 11 Size

Recruiters often get resumes in batches of hundreds. If your resume is on small size paper it is likely to get lost in the pile. If oversized it's likely to get crumpled at the edges, and won't fit in their files.

Typesetting

Modern photocomposition typesetting gives you the clearest, sharpest image, a wide variety of type styles and effects such as italics, bold facing, and book like justified margins. Your original will be on a piece of photographic paper, or you don't have photocomposition. Typesetting is the best resume preparation process, but the most expensive.

Word Processing

The most flexible way to get your resume typed is on a good quality word processor. With word processing, you can make changes almost instantly because your resume will be stored on magnetic disk and the machine will do all the re-typing automatically. A word processing service will usually offer you a variety of type styles in both regular and proportional spacing. You can have bold facing for emphasis, justified margins, and clear, sharp copies.

Typing

Household typewriters and office typewriters with nylon or other cloth ribbons are NOT good for typing the resume you will have printed. If you can't get word processing or typesetting, hire a professional with a high quality office typewriter with a plastic ribbon (usually called a "carbon ribbon").

Printing

Find the best quality offset printing process available. DO NOT make your copies on an office photocopier. Only the personnel office may see the resume you mail. Everyone else may see only a copy of it. Copies of copies quickly become unreadable. Some professionally maintained, extra-high-quality photocopiers are of adequate quality, if you are in a rush. But top quality offset printing is best.

Proofread Your Resume

Whether you typed it yourself or had it written, typed, or typeset. Mistakes on resumes can be embarrassing. Particularly when something obvious such as your name is misspelled. No matter how much you paid someone else to type or write or typeset your resume YOU lose if there is a mistake. So proofread as carefully as possible. Get a friend to help you. Read your draft aloud as your friend checks the proof copy. Then have your friend read aloud while you check. Next, read it letter by letter to check spelling and punctuation.

If you are having it typed or typeset by a resume service or a printer, and you can't bring a friend or take the time during the day to proof it, pay for it and take it home. Proof it there and bring it back later to get it corrected and printed.

RESUME FORMAT
(See samples)

Basic Data

Your name, phone number, and a complete address should be at the top of your resume. (If you are a university student, you should also show your home address and phone number.)

Separate your education and work experience

In general, list your experience first. If you have recently graduated, list your education first, unless your experience is more important than your education. (For example if you have just graduated from a teaching school, have some business experience and are applying for a job in business you would list your business experience first.) If you have two or more years of college, you don't need to list high schools.

Reverse chronological order

To a recruiter your last job and your latest schooling are the most important. So put the last first and list the rest going back in time.

Show dates and locations

Put the dates of your employment and education on the left of the page. Put the names of the companies you worked for and the schools you attended a few spaces to the right of the dates. Put the city and state or city and country where you studied or worked to the right of the page.

Avoid sentences and large blocks of type

Your resume will be scanned, not read. Short, concise phrases are much more effective than long-winded sentences. Keep everything easy to find Avoid paragraphs longer than 6 lines. Never go 10 or more lines in a paragraph. If you have more than 6 lines of information about one job or school, put it in two or more paragraphs.

RESUME CONTENT

Be factual

In many companies inaccurate information on a resume or other application material will get you fired as soon as the inaccuracy is discovered. Protect yourself.

Be positive

You are selling your skills and accomplishments in your resume. If you achieved something, say so. Put it in the best possible light. Don't hold back or be modest, no one else will. But don't exaggerate to the point of misrepresentation.

Be brief

Write down the important (and pertinent) things you have done, but do it in as few words as possible. The shorter your resume is the more carefully it will be examined.

Work experience

Emphasize continued experience in a particular type of function or continued interest in a particular industry. De-emphasize irrelevant positions. Delete positions that you held for less than four months. (Unless you are a very recent college grad or still in school.)

Stress your results

Elaborate on how you contributed to your past employers. Did you increase sales, reduce costs, improve a product, implement a new program? Were you promoted?

Mention relevant skills and responsibilities

Be specific. Slant your past accomplishments toward the type of position that you hope to obtain. Example: Do you hope to supervise people? Then state how many people, performing what function, you have supervised.

Education

Keep it brief if you have more than two years of career experience. Elaborate more if you have less experience. Mention degrees received and any honors or special awards. Note individual courses or research projects that might be relevant for employers. For instance if you are a liberal arts major, be sure to mention courses in such areas as: accounting, statistics, computer programming, or mathematics.

Job objective?

Leave it out. Even if you are certain of exactly the type of job that you desire, the inclusion of a job objective might eliminate you from consideration for other positions that a recruiter feels are a better match for your qualifications.

Personal data

Keep it very brief. Two lines maximum. A one-word mention of commonly practiced activities such as golf, skiing, sailing, chess, bridge, tennis etc. can prove to be a good way to open up a conversation during an interview. Do not include your age, weight, height, etc.

SHOULD YOU HIRE A RESUME WRITER?

Advantages to writing it yourself: If you write reasonably well, there are some advantages to writing your resume yourself. To write it well you will have to review your experience and figure out how to explain your accomplishments in clear, brief phrases. This will help you when you explain your work to interviewers.

If you write your resume, everything in it will be in your own words - it will sound like you. It will say what you want it to say. And you will be much more familiar with the contents. If you are a good writer, know yourself well and have a good idea of what parts of your background employers are looking for, you may be able to write your won resume better than anyone else can. If you write your resume yourself you should have someone who can be objective (preferably not a close relative) review it with you.

When should you have your resume professionally written?

If you have difficulty writing in Resume Style (which is quite unlike normal written language). If you are unsure of which parts of your background you should emphasize, or if you think your resume would make you case better if it did not follow the standard form outlined here or in a book on resumes.

There are two reasons even some professional resume writers we know have had their resumes written with the help of fellow professionals. First, when they need the help of someone who can be objective about their background, and second, when they want an experienced sounding board to help focus their thoughts.

If you decide to hire a resume writer

The best way to choose a writer is by reputation - the recommendation of a friend, a personnel director, your school placement officer or someone else knowledgeable in the field.

You should ask, "If I'm not satisfied with what you write, will you go over it with me and change it?"

You should ask, "How long has the person who will write my resume been writing resumes?"

There is no sure relation between price and quality, except that you are unlikely to get a good writer for less than $50 for an uncomplicated resume and you shouldn't have to pay more than $300 unless your experience is very extensive or complicated. There will be additional charges for printing.

Few resume services will give you a firm price over the phone, simply because some people's resumes are too complicated and take too long to do at any predetermined price. Some services will quote you a price that applies to almost all of their customers. Be sure to do some comparative shopping. Obtain a firm price before you engage their services and find out how expensive minor changes will be.

COVER LETTERS

Always mail a cover letter with your resume In a cover letter you can show an interest in the company that you can't show in a resume. You can point out one or two skills or accomplishments the company can put to good use.

Make it personal

The more personal you can get the better. If someone known to the person you are writing has recommended you contact the company, get permission to include that name in the letter. If you have the name of a person to send the letter to, make sure you have the name spelled correctly and address it directly to that person. Be sure to put the person's name and title on both the letter and envelope. This will ensure that your letter will get through to the proper person, even if a new person now occupies this position. But even if you are addressing it to the "Personnel Director" or the "Hiring Partner," send a letter.

Type cover letters in full. Don't try the cheap and easy ways like photocopying the body of your letter and typing in the inside address and salutation. You will give the impression that you are mailing to a multitude of companies and have no particular interest in any one. Have your letters fully typed and signed with a pen.

Phone

Precede or follow your mailing with a phone call.

Bring extra copies of your resume to the interview

If the person interviewing you doesn't have your resume, be prepared. Carry copies of your own. Even if you have already forwarded your resume be sure to take extra copies to the interview, as someone other than the interviewer(s) might now have the first copy you sent

THE SEATTLE JOB BANK

CHRONOLOGICAL RESUME

(Prepared on office quality typewriter.)

STEVEN M. PHILLIPS

1015 Commonwealth Avenue
Apartment 16
Boston, Massachusetts 02145
Phone: 617/277-1483

Home Address:
507 North 6th Street
Houston, Texas 77024
Phone: 713/461-2341

education
1977-1981 BOSTON UNIVERSITY   BOSTON, MASSACHUSETTS

Candidate for the degree of Bachelor of Arts in June 1981, majoring in Mathematics. Courses include Statistics and Computer Programming. Thesis topic: "New Applications of Co-Linear Coordinates." 3.4 grade point average. Awarded the Elliot Smith Scholarship in 1978.

Treasurer of The Mathematics Club. Responsible for $7,000.00 annual budget. Co-chairperson of Boston University's semi-annual symposium on The Future of Mathematics. Assistant Photography Editor of <u>The Free Press</u>. Exhibitor and prize-winner at local photography shows. Helped to establish university darkroom.

1973-1977 HOUSTON PUBLIC HIGH SCHOOL   HOUSTON, TEXAS

Received High School Diploma in June 1977. Achieved Advance Placement Standing in Calculus and Physics. Academic Honors all terms. Assistant Editor of Year-Book.

experience
summer
1980   DATA PUNCH ASSOCIATES, INC.   NEW YORK, NEW YORK

Mail Clerk and Courier for the Accounting Department. Reorganized mail distribution and sorting system in the department. Delivered sensitive documents to the executive branch.

summers
1978, 1979 HARVEY'S BEEFBURGERS, INC.   HOUSTON, TEXAS

Began work as a dishwasher. Was promoted to short-order cook.

part-time BOSTON UNIVERSITY   BOSTON, MASSACHUSETTS

One of six students invited to tutor for The Department of Mathematics. Also graded student papers and worked as a Research Assistant in Theoretical Calculus.

part-time
1977-1978 BOSTON UNIVERSITY BOOKSTORE   BOSTON, MASSACHUSETTS

Floor and Stockroom Clerk. Responsibilities included arranging merchandise displays, customer service and checking invoices against shipments.

personal
background Enjoy photography, reading science fiction, and playing bridge. Published two articles in mathematics journals.

references Personal references available upon request.

THE SEATTLE JOB BANK

CHRONOLOGICAL RESUME

(Prepared on photo typesetter.)

ROBERT JAMES EDWARDS

70 Highland Avenue
Needham, Massachusetts 02192
Phone: 617-444-8139

business experience

1974-1981   **UNITED PACKAGING CORPORATION**   **BOSTON, MA**

1979-1981   *District Sales Manager.* Improved 28-member sales group from a company rank in the bottom thirty percent to the top twenty percent. Complete responsibility for personnel, including recruiting, hiring and training. Developed a comprehensive sales improvement program and advised its implementation in 8 additional sales districts.

1976-1978   *Marketing Associate*, responsible for research, analysis, and presentation of marketing issues related to long-term corporate strategy. Developed marketing perspective for capital investment opportunities and acquisition candidates, which was instrumental in finalizing decisions to make 2 major acquisitions and to construct a $35 million canning plant.

1974-1976   *Salesman, Paper Division*, responsible for a 4 county territory in central Massachusetts. Increased sales from $700,000 to over $1,050,000 annually in a 15 month period. Developed 6 new accounts with incremental sales potential of $800,000. Only internal candidate selected for new marketing program.

AMERICAN PAPER PRODUCTS, INC.   **NEW YORK, NY**

1973-1974   *Sales Trainee.* Completed the intensive six month training program and was promoted to salesman status. Received The President's Award for superior performance in the sales training program.

HENDRICKSON SPORTING GOODS, INC.   **NEW YORK, NY**

1972   *Assistant Store Manager.* Supervised 6 employees on the evening shift. Handled accounts receivable.

education

1967-1972   **NORTHEASTERN UNIVERSITY**   **BOSTON, MA**

Received Bachelor of Science Degree in Business Administration in June 1972. Varsity Baseball. Financed 50% of educational costs through part-time and co-op program employment.

personal background

Married with two children. Able to relocate. Avid golfer. Excellent health. Active in community activities.

references

Personal references available upon request.

THE SEATTLE JOB BANK

CHRONOLOGICAL RESUME

(Prepared on word processor.)

JOAN M. MORRISON
43 Hilltop Drive
Chicago, Illinois 60612
(312) 312-3123 (home)
(312) 423-4234 (work)

RELATED
EXPERIENCE
1972-Present GREAT LAKES PUBLISHING CO., CHICAGO, ILLINOIS
Operations Supervisor (1976-Present) in the Engineering Division of this major trade publishing house, responsible for maintaining on line computerized customer files, title files, accounts receivable, inventory and sales files.

Organize department activities, establish priorities and train personnel. Provide corporate accounting with monthly reports of sales, earned income from journals, samples, inventory levels/value and sales tax data. Divisional sales average $3 Million annually.

Senior Customer Service Representative (1974-1976) in the Construction Division, answered customer service inquiries regarding orders and accounts receivable, issued return and shortage credits and expedited special sales orders for direct mail and sales to trade schools.

Customer Service Representative (1972-1973), International Division. Same duties as for Construction Division except sales were to retail stores and universities in Europe.

1970-1972 B. DALTON, BOOKSELLER, SALT LAKE CITY, UTAH
Assistant Manager of this retail branch of a major domestic book seller, maintained all paperback inventories at necessary levels, deposited receipts daily and created window displays.

EDUCATION
1966-1970 UNIVERSITY OF MAINE, ORONO, MAINE
Awarded a degree of Bachelor of Arts in French Literature.

LANGUAGES Fluent in French. Able to write in French, German and Spanish.

PERSONAL Willing to travel and relocate, particularly in Europe.

References available upon request.

THE SEATTLE JOB BANK

CHRONOLOGICAL/FUNCTIONAL TWO PAGE RESUME (PAGE ONE)

(Prepared on photo typesetter.)

CHARLES L. PARKHURST
13 River Oaks Circle
Houston, TX 77032
713/832-2184

ACCOMPLISHMENTS

- As Corporate Vice President increased sales of imported products from zero to $2.5 million while new plant was being constructed.

- Invented on-stream waste recovery process which saves $30,000 per year in raw material costs and eliminated need for $150,000 EPA required waste treatment plant.

- Installed computer based training program to handle chemical processing emergencies. Reduced line shut downs 25%.

- Selected site, acquired land, supervised building construction and design, layout, and installation of $6 million in production equipment. Recruited managers to operate this 88,000 square foot facility. This was done on time and under budget.

- As Sales Manager recruited and trained a sales and marketing team that increased volume from $1.8 million to $9.5 million over a 4-year period.

- Developed market for unique bio-chemicals; started and developed marketing program that resulted in $2.3 million in sales.

- Created market demand for bio-chemicals and established a strong customer base resulting in a sales increase from $350,000 to $1.8 million within an 18-month period.

- Developed new quality control techniques for analysis of steroid production intermediates resulting in high product yield.

THE SEATTLE JOB BANK

CHRONOLOGICAL/FUNCTIONAL
TWO PAGE RESUME

PAGE 2

business experience

1968-Present

HOUSTON INTERNATIONAL INDUSTRIES, INC.   HOUSTON, TEXAS

1977-Present   *Back Bay Biologicals, Inc.*   Houston, Texas

President, Back Bay Biologicals; Corporate Vice President, Houston International Industries, Inc.

Have complete responsibility for profit and loss. Prepare strategic plans with corporate staff. Personally supervise finance, marketing, manufacturing, research and personnel functions. Present operational and strategic plans project growth to $8 million with 24% ROI by 1983. Report directly to parent company.

1968-1977   *Prides Crossing Corporation*   Houston, Texas

1974-1977   General Manager-Industrial Division

Responsible for sales and marketing of bio-chemicals to industrial and retail markets. Supervised staff of 18. Prepared short and long-term business plans to meet corporate objectives. Increased sales from $1.8 million to $9.5 million. Reported directly to President.

1970-1974   Sales Manager

Responsible for sales of bio-chemicals to industrial and retail markets. Recruited, trained and supervised sales staff.

1968-1970   Sales Engineer

Developed sales to industrial markets.

1965-1968   **HAMILTON CORPORATION**   DALLAS, TEXAS

Product Manager

Established commercial development of iso-polymers.

education

M.B.A. Evening Program, University of Houston, Houston, TX, 1972.
B.S. in Chemistry, Boston College, Boston, MA, 1960.
Completed many courses in Financial Management, Industrial Marketing, Organic Chemistry, Human Resources, Business Law and Operations Management.

personal

Married, six children. Will travel and relocate. Enjoy horseback riding, sailing, handball, tennis, and golf.

references

References available upon request.

THE SEATTLE JOB BANK

CHRONOLOGICAL RESUME

(Prepared on photo typesetter.)

KATHERINE ELIZABETH BRETTENER
2011 Hill Top View Way
San Francisco, California 94105
415/532-4731

EXPERIENCE

ULTRASHEEN STONE JEWELER   San Francisco, California
1976-Present
Senior Designer
Created ultrasheen stone jewelry for exhibits at Rotunda Gallery, Sak's Fifth Avenue, New York; San Regret Gallery, Los Angeles (1980); Institute of Contemporary Art, San Francisco (1979); Weatherway Gallery, and Smith Street Shop, Seattle, Washington (1978).

AMERICAN ARTISTIC FOUNDATION   San Francisco, California
1975
Organizational Assistant
Gathered material for presentation of Art Day Catalog at the American Artistic Foundation. Accepted by juried committee to present work in Art Day Catalog.

DIABLO PHOTO STUDIO   San Francisco, California
1974
Promotional Assistant
Did public relations work for industrial and commercial photographers. Sought corporate accounts for on-location product photography.

GALILEO GALLERY   Seattle, Washington
1973
Retail Sales Representative
Assisted in art displays and sold merchandise.

EDUCATION

UNIVERSITY OF CALIFORNIA, Berkeley   Berkeley, California
Awarded PhD Degree in Existential Philosophy in 1978.

STANFORD UNIVERSITY   Stanford, California
Awarded Bachelor of Arts Degree in Art History in 1974. Curriculum emphasis in Modern European Period.

BACKGROUND

Will travel. Enjoy all aspects of performing and creative art, tennis, and yoga.

References available upon request.

THE SEATTLE JOB BANK

CHRONOLOGICAL RESUME

(Prepared on word processor.)

JAMES WASHINGTON WHITE, JR.

U.S. Address:
486 East 77th Street
New York, New York 10021
(212) 212-2121

Jamaican Address:
Room 1234
Playboy, Jamaica
Doctor's Beach, Jamaica
(809) 326-1312

experience

1974-present   PLAYBOY, JAMAICA LTD.   DOCTOR'S BEACH, JAMAICA
<u>Resident Engineer</u> for this publicly owned resort with main offices in Chicago, Illinois responsibilities include:

Maintain electrical generating and distribution equipment.

Supervise an eight-member staff in maintenance of refrigeration equipment, power and light generators, water purification plant, and general construction machinery.

1972-1974   NIGRIL BEACH HOTEL   NIGRIL BEACH, JAMAICA
<u>Resident Engineer</u> for a privately-held resort, assigned total responsibility for facility generating equipment.

Directed maintenance, operation and repair of diesel generating equipment.

1970-1972   Directed overhaul of turbo generating equipment in two Mid-Western localities and assisted in overhaul of a turbo generating unit in Mexico.

1965-1970   CAPITAL CITY ELECTRIC   WASHINGTON, D.C.
<u>Service Engineer</u> for the power generation service division of this regional power company, supervised the overhaul, maintenance and repair of large generators and associated auxiliary equipment.

other experience   A Night File Supervisor for Columbia Mutual Life Insurance Company (1963-1965) and an Apprentice Welder at the Potomac Naval Shipyard from 1961-1962.

Volunteer Co-ordinator Washington D.C. NAACP 1969; Activities Co-chairman 1968

education

1962-1965   FRANKLIN INSTITUTE   BALTIMORE, MARYLAND
Awarded a degree of Associate of Engineering. Concentration in Mechanical Power Engineering Technology.

personal   Willing to travel and relocate.
Interested in sailing, scuba diving, deep sea fishing.

References available upon request.

THE SEATTLE JOB BANK

CHRONOLOGICAL RESUME

(Prepared on photo typesetter.)

NATHAN JAMES FREDERICK, III

10012 Ocean View Park
Los Angeles, California 90012
213/744-8112

business experience

1978 to present   **PACIFIC COMPUTER LEASING**   Los Angeles, CA

Manager of Debt Placement
- Responsible for developing and maintaining bank and institutional debt sources.
- Structured leases for maximum tax advantages.
- Have documented and closed $120,000,000 of secured loans.
- Work closely with investment bankers and bank and institutional funding sources.

1971-1978   **PRIME COMPUTER, INC.**   Natick, MA

Customer Finance Marketing Manager, North America
- Responsible for the profitable management of finance lease and tax exempt installment programs in the United States and Mexico used by government and business.
- Implementation of the programs through field based customer financing representatives. Insured financing arrangements met FASB requirements for sale recognition by vendor.
- Made certain pricing and documentation were suitable for sale of portfolio to funding institutions. Typical transaction exceeded $750,000.

1968-1971   **COPPERBOTTOM INFORMATION SYSTEMS**   Philadelphia, PA

11 70-5 71   Manager of Marketing Proposal Analysis   Atlanta, GA
- Advised field sales force in the initial stages of proposals with emphasis on the financial aspects of operating and finance leases, installment sales, and multi-party transactions.

1 70-11 70   Sectional Revenue Manager   Winston-Salem, NC
- Achieved planned lease purchase revenue mix, by appropriate pricing policies and financial agreements with customers.

6 68-1 70   Sales Finance   Baltimore, MD
- Implemented and administered Copperbottom's finance lease program. Educated field sales personnel in financial plans. Handled administration of equipment add-ons, replacements, handled contract amendments.

1962-1968   **BAYBANK, N.A.**   Portland, OR
- Branch Manager responsible for all aspects of the day-to-day operation of a branch bank.

education

1956-1960   **BABSON COLLEGE**   Wellesley, MA
- Bachelor of Science in Business Administration with a major in financial management, minor in mathematics.

languages   Fluent in Spanish.

references   References will be supplied upon request.

THE SEATTLE JOB BANK

CHRONOLOGICAL RESUME

(Prepared on photo typesetter.)

KENNETH WANG
412 Country Club Lane
Albany, New York 12207
518/371-4387

EXPERIENCE

1977-Present   **THE CENTER COMPANY**, Albany, NY

Systems Analyst, design systems for the manufacturing unit. Specifically, physical inventory, program specifications, studies of lease buy decisions, selection of hardware for the IBM 9999, 1010, and Alpha Communications, and supervise the outside contractors and inside users. Wrote On Site Computer Terminal Operators Manual. Modelled product mix problems with the LAPSP (Logistical Alternative Product Synthesis Programming).

As *Industrial Engineer* from February 1979 to February 1980, computerized system design. Evaluated manufacturing operations operator efficiency productivity index and budget allocations. Analyzed material waste and recommended solutions.

ADDITIONAL EXPERIENCE

1975-1976   *Graduate Research Assistant* at New York State Institute of Technology.
1970-1972   *Graduate Teaching Assistant* at Salem State University.

EDUCATION

1974-1976   NEW YORK STATE INSTITUTE OF TECHNOLOGY, Albany, NY
M.S. in Operations Research. G.P.A.: 3.6. Graduate courses included Advanced Location and Queueing Theories, Forecasting, Inventory and Material Flow Systems, Linear and Nonlinear Determination Models, Engineering Economics and Integer Programming.

1972-1974   M.S. in Information and Computer Sciences. G.P.A.: 3.8. Curriculum included Digital Computer Organization & Programming, Information Structure & Process, Mathematical Logic, Computer Systems, Logic Design and Switching Theory.

1970-1972   SALEM STATE UNIVERSITY, Salem, OR
M.A. in Mathematics. G.P.A.: 3.6.

1963-1967   ALL KOREA UNIVERSITY, Seoul, Korea
B.S. in Engineering.

AFFILIATIONS

Member of the American Institute of Computer Programmers, Association for Computing Machinery and the Operations Research Society of America.

PERSONAL

Married, three dependents. Able to relocate.

THE SEATTLE JOB BANK

CHRONOLOGICAL RESUME

(Prepared on photo typesetter.)

ALLAN K. SIMPSON
89 Village Way
Dobbs Ferry, New York 10522
914/314-3713

experience

1976-present   **WALL STREET SECURITIES**
                   PROCESSING SERVICES INC.   **NEW YORK, NY**

Vice President in charge of operations. Adminster personnel policies, salary reviews. Prepare and implement budgets. Oversee and coordinate user departments and outside customers, production, request and problems. Produce and maintain all schedules and related documentation. Supervise 21 individuals who are involved in utilizing a Digital 9999 computer system on a 24-hour basis.

1970-1976   **MANHATTAN CLEARING CORPORATION**   **NEW YORK, NY**

As Vice President in charge of Clearing Operations, prepared and implemented five department budgets. Oversaw money management, accounting, billing and dividend control. Implemented procedures to account for lost, stolen and counterfeit securities, reviewed bank accounts, suspenses of monies and billing of customers. Supervised 97 individuals in daily clearance of securities and monies valued at 35-60 million dollars. Documented job descriptions and reorganized personnel into better functioning departments. Coordinated customer requests and complaints to ensure proper evaluation and follow-up.

1968-1970   **FIRST FEDERAL NATIONAL BANK**   **CHICAGO, IL**
                   MUTUAL FUNDS OPERATION

As Senior Operator, prepared data and entry controls as input into the Shareholder Accounting System of over 55 mutual funds. Operated and maintained programs of electronic accounting machines, reproducers, interpreters and other related equipment. Wrote and maintained programs for IBM 360 computer system. Placed on special assignment for implementation of data entry controls of the credit card system.

education   **UNIVERSITY OF ILLINOIS**   **CHAMPAIGN, IL**

Awarded B.S. degree in Business Studies with a minor in Computer Science.

affiliations   Member of the New York Chapter of the Securities Operations Association. Member of the National Data Processing Management Association.

voluntary activity   Chairman of the Board, the Eastern Square Community Development Corporation, a bi-racial organization working to revitalize a neighborhood shopping district.

THE SEATTLE JOB BANK

FUNCTIONAL RESUME

(Prepared on photo typesetter.)

JOHN SINGLETON COPLEY
420 Boylston Street
Pittsburgh, Pennsylvania 15234
412/323-3491

Solid background in plate making, separations, color matching, background definition, printing, mechanicals, color corrections, and supervision of personnel. A highly motivated manager, adept problem-solver and effective communicator. Proven ability to:

- Create Commercial Graphics
- Produce Embossing Drawings
- Color Separate
- Analyze Consumer Acceptance

- Meet Graphic Deadlines
- Control Quality
- Resolve Printing Problems
- Expedite Printing Operations

Qualifications

Printing — Black and white and color. Can judge acceptability of color reproduction by comparing it with original. Can make four or five color corrections on all media. Have long developed ability to restyle already reproduced four-color art work. Can create perfect tone for black and white match fill-ins for resume cover letters.

Customer Relations — Work well with customers to assure specifications are met and customers are satisfied. Can guide work through entire production process and strike a balance between technical printing capabilities and need for customer approval.

Management — Schedule work to meet deadlines. Direct staff in production procedures. Control budgets, maintain quality control from inception of project through final approval for printing.

Specialties   Make silk screen overlays and overlays for a multitude of processes. Velo bind. GBC bind, perfect bind. Gold leaf embossing, silver inlay stamping. Have knowledge to prepare posters, flyers, business cards and personalized stationery.

Personnel Supervision – Foster an atmosphere that encourages highly talented artists to balance high level creativity with a maximum of production. Have managed a group of over 20 photographers, developers, plate etchers, checkers and artists. Met or beat production deadlines. Am continually instructing new employees, apprentices and students in both artistry and technical operations.

Experience

Assistant Production Manager, Artsign Digraphics, Erie, PA (1952-Present) Part time.
Professor of Graphic Arts, Pennsylvania College of Fine Arts, Pittsburgh, PA (1950-Present)

Education

Massachusetts Conservatory of Art PhD 1950

THE SEATTLE JOB BANK

GENERAL MODEL FOR A COVER LETTER

>   Your
>   Address
>
>   Date
>
> Contact Person Name
> Title
> Company
> Address
>
> Dear Mr.(Ms.) _____:
>
>   Immediately explain why your background makes you the best candidate for the position that you are applying for. Keep the first paragraph short and hard-hitting.
>
>   Detail what you could contribute to this company. Show how your qualifications will benefit this firm. Remember to keep this letter short; few recruiters will read a cover letter longer than a half-a-page.
>
>   Describe your interest in the corporation. Subtly emphasize your knowledge about this firm (the result of your research effort) and your familiarity with the industry. It is common courtesy to act extremely eager to work for any company that you interview.
>
>   In the closing paragraph you should specifically request an interview. Include your phone number and the hours when you can best be reached. Alternatively, you might prefer to mention that you will follow-up with a phone call (to arrange an interview at a mutually convenient time) within the next several days.
>
>   Sincerely yours,
>
>   (signature)
>
>   Full Name (typed)
>
> Enc. Resume

THE SEATTLE JOB BANK

COVER LETTER

411 Lookout Avenue
Apartment 48c
Boston, Massachusetts 02131

March 15, 19__

Ms. Andrea Larson
Sales Manager
Northern Products Corporation
412 Elm River Expressway
Denver, Colorado 80201

Dear Ms. Larson:

I seek a position as a sales representative with Northern Products and I offer, in return, thorough industry experience and more than eleven years of solid practical background in sales.

As a sample of sales achievement, I increased my personal monthly gross sales volume to a point where it tripled the combined sales of three other full-time representatives for one ski manufacturer. Also, I have won numerous international and domestic sales awards.

As an experienced sales representative, I have succeeded in improving area or regional sales by utilizing a combination of aggressiveness, enthusiasm, and persistence. I have been able to bring out these traits in those whom I have hired and trained in my capacity as National Sales Instructor for two companies.

I feel that your new line of fiberglass competition skis offer an unbeatable price/performance combination for the serious skier. I am firmly convinced that I can improve your market penetration in the lucrative Upstate New York Area at least to a top five position.

I am an avid skier. As such, I am familiar with not only the technical terms involved, but with the types of equipment available and the extent to which it is marketed.

I look forward to hearing from you.

         Sincerely,

         Wayne L. Swanson

Enc. Resume

THE SEATTLE JOB BANK

COVER LETTER

49 Smith Park Circle
Houston, Texas 77031

October 5, 19__

Mr. Clinton P. Thomas
Vice President and Director of Personnel
Riverbay Fire Insurance Group
Riverbay Plaza
Houston, Texas 77035

Dear Mr. Thomas:

I am the career oriented individual who can successfully provide technical direction and training to pension analysts in connection with FKLE system.

My major and most recent background is directly involved in the administration of pension and profit sharing plans with TRMZ. Furthermore, my extensive experience both as a Group Pension Pre-Scale Underwriter and as a Pension Underwriter involves data processing knowledge and overall pension administration.

A prime function of mine is decision making with reference to group pension business. You specifically seek an individual who can recommend changes and/or new procedures of plan administration and maintenance plus assistance in development of pension administration kits for use by the field force at Riverbay. I feel that I possess the ability to fulfill your need dramatically.

I would welcome the practical opportunity to work directly with general agents and plan trustees in qualifying, revising and requalifying pension and profit sharing plans required by TRMZ. You will note in my resume my background in working with others in both an advisory and shirt-sleeve capacity.

I look forward to hearing from you.

Sincerely,

Samuel A. Waters

Enc. Resume

THE SEATTLE JOB BANK

COVER LETTER

1012 Winding Hill Road
Newark, New Jersey 07101

December 10, 19__

Mr. Daniel Wentworth
Personnel Manager
Mitchell & Brothers Engineering Services, Inc.
Central Park Square Building
New York, New York 10019

Dear Mr. Wentworth:

My diversity as well as my depth of engineering experience in the wastewater treatment field could prove to be a particularly strong asset for Mitchell & Brothers given the firm's current and continued commitment to being a pioneering innovator in the engineering and construction of wastewater treatment facilities.

I offer an extensive background in investigating, reporting and designing multimillion dollar wastewater treatment facilities, pumping facilities and sewer lines in New Jersey and in Puerto Rico. In addition I have experience in coordinating engineering services during construction of sewers and pumping facilities in Hawaii.

One of my basic strengths is my ability to act as liason for diverse engineering and non-engineering individuals and groups to keep a project on schedule and in line with funding constraints.

I have come to a point in my career where I desire to expand into areas where I might utilize over 8 years of solid engineering experience. These areas include hazardous waste treatment, industrial wastewater and water treatment, and water supply.

I will be glad to furnish any additional information you desire. You may reach me during the day at 201/576-1100. I look forward to hearing from you.

Sincerely,

John T. Lent

Enc. Resume

THE SEATTLE JOB BANK

COVER LETTER

>1015 Commonwealth Avenue
>Apartment 16
>Boston, Massachusetts 02145
>
>February 15, 19__

Mr. Clark T. Johnson
Vice-President/Human Resources
Boston City Bank Corporation
110 Milk Street
Boston, Massachusetts 02114

Dear Mr. Johnson:

    Having majored in Mathematics at Boston University, where I also worked as a Research Assistant, I am confident that I would make a very successful Research Trainee in your Economics Research Department.

    In addition to my strong background in mathematics, I also offer significant business experience, having worked in a data processing firm, a bookstore, and a restaurant. I am sure that my courses in statistics and computer programming would prove particularly useful in the position of Research Trainee.

    I am attracted to City Bank by your recent rapid growth and the superior reputation of your Economic Research Department. After studying different commercial banks, I have concluded that City Bank will be in a strong competitive position to benefit from upcoming changes in the industry, such as the phasing out of Regulation Q.

    I would like to interview with you at your earliest convenience. I am best reached between 3 and 5 p.m. at 277-1483.

>Sincerely yours,
>
>Steven M. Phillips

Enc. Resume

THE SEATTLE JOB BANK

COVER LETTER

311 East Wind Lake Towers
8355 Western Avenue
Minneapolis, Minnesota 55431

July 10, 19__

Mr. Jorge Melendez
President
Thompson Associates, Inc.
411 Longview Parkway
Chicago, Illinois 60611

Dear Mr. Melendez:

Can you utilize the talents of a competent, motivated, and well-organized Management Generalist who is thoroughly accomplished in accounting procedures, systems analysis, office administration, and personnel evaluation?

Thompson Associates' rapid growth in addition to the fast-paced environment of the software industry may have created general business needs best handled by a Management Generalist familiar with the software industry. A Management Generalist could perform tasks that would allow senior engineers to focus exclusively on creating the innovative software packages that have brought Thompson Associates the success it enjoys today.

I can offer a strong, multifaceted business background in which I have achieved notable success in communication, financial management, procedures analysis, and personnel development.

Can we meet to discuss what I might be able to contribute to Thompson Associates? You may reach me by calling 612/395-5847 or by sending a note to the above address. I look forward to hearing from you. Thank you for your consideration.

Sincerely,

Nancy L. Mellon

Enc. Resume

GENERAL MODEL
FOR A FOLLOW-UP LETTER

                                          Your
                                          Address

                                          Date

Contact Person Name
Title
Company
Address

Dear Mr.(Ms.) _____:

    Remind the interviewer of the position for which you were interviewed, as well as the date. Thank him (her) for the interview.

    Confirm your interest in the opening and the organization. Use specifics to emphasize both that you have researched the firm in detail and considered how you would fit into the company and the position.

    Like in your cover letter, emphasize one or two of your strongest qualifications and slant them toward the various points that the interviewer considered the most important for the position. Keep the letter brief, a half-page is plenty.

    If appropriate, close with a suggestion for further action, such as a desire to have additional interviews. Mention your phone number and the hours that you can best be reached. Alternatively, you may prefer to mention that you will follow-up with a phone call in several days.

                                        Sincerely yours,

                                        (signature)

                                      Your Full Name (typed)
                                      Phone number (if not in text)

In addition to this book, Bob Adams, Inc. publishes a number of other career and job-search related titles.

Knock 'em Dead with Great Answers to Tough Interview Questions (3rd. Edition) by Martin John Yate

When Martin John Yate wrote *Knock 'Em Dead with Great Answers to Tough Interview Questions* almost two years ago, it was an instant success. The critical acclaim was from far and wide, and bookstores reported sellouts. Job seekers everywhere were learning how to interview more effectively.

192 pages, $6.95

Now, Yate has revised and expanded his book. The third edition of *Knock 'em Dead* includes a new section with questions from today's toughest interviewers. Yate shows the interviewee how to get behind the interviewer's questions, and to discover the traits that he or she is looking for.

"Expressing your answers in ways that will reveal your real business acumen and potential" is the key, Yate advises. "There are definitely convincing responses, responses that will get you the job you want and deserve."

Resumes that Knock 'em Dead
by Martin John Yate

"This is the best book on how to write a resume ever written."

- Jack Bilson, Manager of Professional Employment, Unisys Corporation

Every single resume in *Resumes that Knock 'em Dead* was used by a real job applicant within the last eighteen months to successfully obtain a job.

Many of the resumes shown were successfully used to change careers; others resulted in dramatically higher salaries. Some produced both. For example, a man working as a $6-an-hour welder used his resume to obtain a $70,000-a-year sales position.

200 pages, $7.95

To serve as broad an audience as possible, Yate carefully chose resumes for the 150 most commonly-sought positions on all levels.

Yate also reviews the marks of a great resume -- what type of resume is right for each applicant, what goes in, what stays out, and why.

No other book provides the hard facts for producing an exemplary resume. No other book can produce resumes that knock 'em dead.

Careers and the MBA
edited by Gigi Ranno

"Long considered the MBA's Bible."

- The Wall Street Journal

Careers and the MBA is the leading career reference guide for MBA students as well as graduates.

Each edition of this annually updated publication provides in-depth corporate profiles of more than 100 leading recruiters of MBAs. These profiles give readers up-to-date, specific information on the companies that can best use their professional education.

220 pages, $14.95

Feature articles by leaders in the business world address issues that affect virtually all business school graduates, whatever their specialization. Also, industry reports, written by specialists in various fields, provide readers with insightful overviews of 23 major industries, with an emphasis on MBA careers. The last chapter provides the addresses of 700 companies that are currently recruiting MBAs.

Careers and the College Grad
edited by Gigi Ranno

"Excellent! I was impressed with both the quality and the approach. The magazine itself, as well as the articles, is impressive!"

- Athena Consantine, Director, Office of University Placement and Career Services, Columbia University

Careers and the College Grad is a complete annual resource guide addressing the particular career interests of undergraduates. It contains 128 pages of valuable career advice -- company profiles, interviews with leaders in the business community and in-depth industry reports by experts in each field.

128 pages, $12.95

Careers and the College Grad covers all of the major industries that are of interest to students. It also gives special attention to the industries with extremely selective recruitment programs such as investment banking, commercial banking, and management consulting.

In addition, the magazine offers detailed information about the companies leading recruiters of college students. Information includes the name of the people to contact, phone numbers, address, company profiles, business activities, and most importantly, the specific functions for which each company will be hiring this year.

Careers and the College Grad also includes feature articles, written by leading executives. These features are intended to impart knowledge and advice to those about to enter the business world.

Also featured are detailed industry reports, offering college students an overview of a particular field -- its basic structure, important trends, possible job paths, keys to success, advancement opportunities, and future industry directions.

In addition, a section on job search techniques gives college students specific advice on all the key steps of the search process.

The Job Search Handbook
The Basics of the Professional Job Search
by John Noble, Associate Director of Career Services, Harvard University

At last, here is a concise, easy to read handbook for anyone trying to find the right job fast!

John Noble, Associate Director of Career Services at Harvard University, has identified the most important

144 pages, $6.95

elements of a successful job hunt and condensed them into an easily accessible, no-nonsense primer that allows job seekers to lay the foundations of a professional job search immediately -- and spend less time following unproductive leads.

Mr. Noble, previously an editor of the nationwide *Job Bank* series of employment reference guides, offers a straightforward, concise job search text. The trim 5 x 8 format sets the book apart from those long-winded and repetitive job search titles, and the author's outstanding credentials target the book immediately to its vast audience: first-time entrants into the job market, those looking for a new job in a new field, and the middle level professional looking to take the next step up.

The Job Bank Series

How do you find out where to get the jobs? Here's what you need to know:

o Full name, address, and telephone number of firm.
o Contact name for professional hiring.
o Thorough description of firm's primary business.
o Listings of common positions filled, educational backgrounds sought, and fringe benefits offered.
o An industry cross-index that allows you to pinpoint employers in your particular field.
o Special chapters that provide tips on how to go about your job search and how to create resumes and cover letters that will make you stand out from the crowd.

There are now 17 *Job Bank* books, each covering a key U.S. job market with comprehensive and up-to-date information for every type of job hunter. Each book is a complete research tool, providing the necessary guidance for every step of the job search, from career choice to the initial contact to the final follow up.

Recent *Job Bank* Titles:

Atlanta Job Bank, 2nd ed.
168 pp., $10.95

Boston Job Bank, 6th ed.
300 pp., $12.95

Chicago Job Bank
300 pp., $12.95

Dallas Job Bank
276 pp., $12.95

Denver Job Bank, 2nd ed.
300 pp., $12.95

Detroit Job Bank
276 pp., $12.95

Florida Job Bank, 2nd ed.
300 pp., $12.95

Houston Job Bank
276 pp., $12.95

Los Angeles Job Bank
240 pp., $10.95

Minneapolis Job Bank, 2nd ed.
300 pp., $12.95

New York Job Bank, 5th ed.
420 pp., $12.95

Ohio Job Bank, 2nd ed.
180 pp., $10.95

Philadelphia Job Bank
204 pp., $10.95

St. Louis Job Bank
276 pp., $12.95

San Francisco Job Bank
276 pp., $12.95

Seattle Job Bank
276 pp., $12.95

Washington D.C. Job Bank, 3rd ed.
216 pp., $10.95

And, coming in April, 1989:

**The Harvard Guide to Careers
in Mass Media**
With Special Insider's Tips from the Worlds of Advertising, Film, Journalism, Publishing, Public Relations, Radio, Recording, and Television

by John Noble, Associate Director of Career Services, Harvard University

Thousands upon thousands of job seekers have entertained the thought of starting a career in one of the high-visibility fields that make up today's mass media. Unfortunately, this employment area represents not only many of the most glamorous jobs in the country -- but also some of the most potentially dangerous traps awaiting any job hunter.

John Noble, Associate Director of Career Services at Harvard University, and author of the successful *Job Search Handbook*, here offers the definitive guide to breaking into the most competitive job market of them all.

Each chapter in *The Harvard Guide to Careers in Mass Media* contains:

o   An industry profile that describes the current state and structure of a given field. A career profile section that describes various positions available in that area

o   Information about current salary ranges.

o   Industry specific job hunting tips and strategies.

o   A real-life case study outlining the methods that were used in a successful job hunt.

The Harvard Guide to Careers in Mass Media is an indispensable, authoritative guide that meets the needs of a vast audience.

To obtain a copy of any of the above books, check your local bookstore.

To order directly, please call 1-800 USA-JOBS. (In Massachusetts, 617/268-9570)

or write to:

Bob Adams, Inc.,
840 Summer Street,
Boston MA 02127.